Christmas in the Family

Isabel Marion

Christmas in the Family

Floris Books

Photographs by Paul Bock
Colour illustrations by Vivienne Cardwell
Line drawings by the author

First published in 2006 by Floris Books

British Library CIP Data available

ISBN-10 0-86315-563-4
ISBN-13 978-086315-563-5

Produced by Polskabook in Poland

Contents

Introduction

The festive season of Christmas is always an important and memorable part of childhood.

For parents it can be a stressful time in today's fast-moving world. The prospect of making cards and presents, doing home baking and preparing the house can be a bit daunting. But in my own experience (both from childhood and as a parent of five), creative work as a family can be both enjoyable and peaceful. Children blossom when involved in satisfying and manageable craftwork and baking, especially when the results have a practical use. As children grow older it is rewarding to see their growing ability, imagination and confidence.

This book has suggestions for turning Christmas into a meaningful and unforgettable festival.

Isabel Marion

Advent

Advent traditionally starts on the fourth Sunday before Christmas Day.

It is wonderful for the children to be woken up on Advent Sunday with the first verse of the Advent carol "People Look East." On getting up they find the Advent calendar in place, and vases of evergreen around the house — fresh and bare, or with a single star. At breakfast the first candle is lit on the Advent wreath and the time of preparation begins.

It can be a rewarding experience to find time during Advent to sit down with the children and teach them various crafts: making decorations, Christmas cards, and most enjoyable for them, baking. It is of great value to the children if they can learn to make simple gifts for their family, teachers and friends. The pleasure in giving is then much increased. Children can be surprisingly capable and imaginative. (Adults who are not used to craft work will be harder to teach then children.) However it is important to choose a craft suitable to the age and ability of the child.

As Advent progresses the evergreen fills up with decorations. Children particularly appreciate having their own branch in their room to decorate as they please. Each Sunday a new verse is added to the Advent carol, and a new candle lit on the Advent wreath. This, and the daily opening of the calendar, give a strong visual impression of the passing of time.

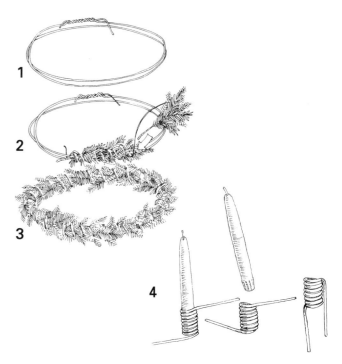

Advent wreath

❖ *thick wire (2 mm, $^1/_{16}$ in) for the hoop
thin wire (1 mm, $^1/_{32}$ in) for the
    candle-holders
sprigs of green fir
waxed thread or string
four candles
a blue ribbon*

1 Take a piece of thick wire the length of which is more than twice the circumference of the Advent wreath, to make a double hoop. Twist the ends firmly together.
2 Cover the frame with greenery. Start by making a foundation with larger twigs, 20–25 cm (8–10 in). Lay the bottom of the first stem against the hoop and bind it on with the waxed thread or fine string. Lay the next twig underneath the first so that it is overlapped by the first and bind it on. Continue in this way so that the wreath gradually increases in thickness.
3 After the first round use smaller sprigs which are less stiff and more easily bound on. For the last round use short beautiful sprigs to give a smooth and even effect.
4 For each of the four candle-holders take a piece of thin wire and wind it several times round the bottom of a candle and then bend the two ends down.

Place the candle-holders on four points of the wreath making sure that they don't disappear into the greenery but remain visible. Bend the protruding ends of wire round the bottom of the wreath.

Cut the blue ribbon in two equal lengths. Tie the ends of both ribbons on to the wreath midway between the candles.

Suspend the Advent wreath by the ribbon. If it is not to be hung the blue ribbon can be wound around the wreath as a decoration.

Advent bough

❖ *some thin, supple, evergreen branches,*
  approximately 60 cm (24 in) long
  strong thread or tape
  small clippings of long-lasting evergreen
    (such as juniper) or treated greenery
  strong glue or glue gun
  dried white flowers
  dried dark brown foliage
  gold sprayed foliage/berries
  whole nuts
  cinnamon sticks
  dried slices of orange/lemon

1 Strip the branches of leaves and arrange the them so the fattest part is
nearest the centre and the thin,
curved end at the outside.
2 Decide on the length of bough
(allow for the ends to be looped back).
Using a strong thread or tape, bind
the twigs together, starting form the
middle.

3 Tie the two middle threads together
securely. Use the end of the threads to
form a loop by bending the thin ends
of the twigs back and tying them
firmly on the bough.
4 Start decorating the bough with the
small springs of greenery, arranged
symmetrically. The sprigs can either be
held down by slipping the stems
under the existing threads, or they can
be tide on with new threads. Do not
fill the bough with too much greenery.
5 Add the remaining stem decorations
in the same way, and then glue on the
nuts, spices and dried fruit. Allow the
glue to dry before hanging.

1

2

3

4

Reusable Advent calendars

These are a lot of work, but well worth it as the children enjoy remembering more and more of the pictures as the years go by. Adults often feel children will be bored with the same calendar every year, but young children benefit from repetition; and just as they love to hear a particular story again and again, they also love to have the festivals celebrated in the same way year in year out. When they wake up on Advent Sunday and see the calendar once more in its place, their faces light up as if greeting a lost friend once more. Children particularly appreciate the artistic efforts of their parents, but if there is no one in the family who can draw, effective calendars can also be made from art cards.

❖ *dark mounting card*
   ruler
   sharp Stanley knife
   drawing materials or suitable art cards
   glue
   gold/silver pens
   gold paper

Design the front of the calendar on a scrap paper. If art cards are being used, the picture on the card can suggest the shape of the door (try to keep the shapes fairly simple as this will make cutting easier). The length of Advent varies from year to year from a minimum of 22 days to a maximum of 28 days. Decide when the final door is to be opened, either on Christmas Eve, or on Christmas morning (in which case 29 doors will be needed. The doors can be numbered, or they can have stars on them. On the years where Advent is shorter, two doors can be opened on selected days.

Transfer the design onto the mounting card with lead pencil. First score the markings gently with the Stanley knife before cutting through the card. A lot of pressure is needed to cut through the mounting card, but ensure there is newspaper underneath the card to protect the cutting surface. When cutting a straight line, always lean the knife against a ruler for accuracy.

As each door is removed, carefully pencil the number on the back corresponding to the design. This is particularly important if many doors have a similar shape.

For an art card calendar, it is easiest to place the card underneath the window and gently pencil the shape of the window onto the card. Remove the card and cut around the marked pencil line (ensuring a small border is left for gluing.) The pencil markings can then be rubbed off the card. Glue sparingly around the border and stick onto the back of the mounting card.

For hand drawn pictures, a whole sheet of paper can be placed underneath the mounting card and the windows spaces can be pencilled in. The sheet can then be removed and the pencilled spaces coloured in. Be sure to colour a little beyond the pencilled mark . This will give a neater finish.

Door "handles" can be made by twisting a strip of gold paper into a loop and sticking down the ends with strong glue on to the door.

Aniseed springerle

This traditional German recipe is made using wood or clay moulds. The cookies should be made well in advance of Christmas, as they can take two to six weeks to soften.

❖ *2 eggs*
  200 g (7 oz) icing sugar/powdered sugar (sifted)
  1 teaspoon natural vanilla essence
  275 g (10 oz) plain flour
  ¼ teaspoon baking powder
  5 g (2 tablespoons) whole aniseed
  Icing sugar/powdered sugar to roll out

Line two baking trays with baking parchment/baking paper. Sprinkle aniseed evenly over paper on both trays. Set aside. Beat eggs until frothy. Add vanilla essence. Slowly add icing sugar/powdered sugar and beat until creamy. Add baking powder to flour, and then gradually stir in the flour to the egg mixture. Knead in the last of the flour.

Using icing sugar/powdered sugar, roll out dough a little less than 1 cm (just over ¼ in) thick. Cut dough into strips and then crossways to form approximate squares. These squares should be about the same size, or slightly smaller than the moulds. If the dough is sticky, gently rub a little icing sugar/powdered sugar over the surface of the square before lifting it up and pressing it face down into the mould. The dough can be "hammered" into the mould, using finger tips, to get a clear impression. This will spread and thin the dough out a little. Remove dough from the mould and trim the edges as desired. Place the dough biscuit on top of the aniseed, so that the aniseed will bake into the bottom of the cookie.

When the trays are both full, leave them to stand for 24 hours at room temperature before baking.

When the cookies are ready for baking, pre-heat the oven and set at Gas Mark 2, (150°C, 300°F). Bake cookies for 30 minutes, they should come out whitish, and not brown.

Store the springerle in a large bowl uncovered, and leave the bowl in a cool place (not the fridge) until the cookies soften.

Recipe makes approximately 40.

People Look East

1 Peo-ple, look East. The time is near Of the crown-ing of___ the
year. Make your house fair as you are a-ble, Trim___ the hearth, and set___ the
ta-ble. Peo-ple, look East, and sing to-day: Love the Guest is on the way.

Peo-ple, look East,_____ Love the Guest is on the way.

Peo-ple, look East, Love the Guest is on the way.

2. Furrows, be glad. Though earth be bare
   One more seed is planted there:
   Give up your strength the seed to nourish,
   That in course the flower may flourish.
   People look ... Love the Rose ...
3. Birds, though ye long have ceased to build.
   Guard the nest that must be filled.
   Even the hour when wings are frozen
   He for fledging-time has chosen.
   People look ... Love the Bird ...

4. Stars, keep the watch. When night is dim
   One more light the bowl shall brim.
   Shining beyond the frosty weather.
   Bright as sun and moon together.
   People look ... Love the Star ...
5 Angels, announce to man and beast
   Him who cometh from the East.
   Set every peak and valley humming
   With the word, the Lord is coming.
   People look ... Love the Lord ...

Double-sided goldfoil decoration

❖ *double-sided gold/coloured foil*
  scissors
  ruler
  glue

Measure and cut out a square of foil.
1 Make creases by folding the square in half from top to bottom, from side to side, and from corner to corner in both directions, opening the foil out between each fold.
2 Fold all four corners to the centre and then open the square out again.
3 Fold the top edge down, and the bottom edge up to meet at the centre line. Repeat for the side edges.
4 Make four small cuts as shown.
5 Fold the cut corners inward.
6 Narrow the points of the star by folding the edges inward once more.

Variations can be created by sticking two stars together to form an eight-pointed star. The stars can be of different sizes and/or reversed colouring. A star centre can also be created by folding the foil together using the creases below, and then cutting a V-shape into the folded point (as for the next star). The foil should then be opened and the folding continued.

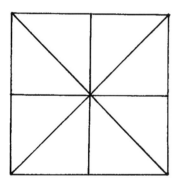

1

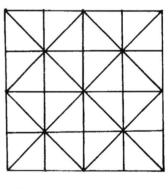

2

3

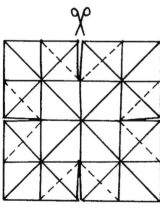

4

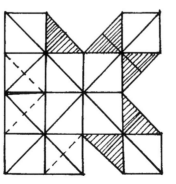

5

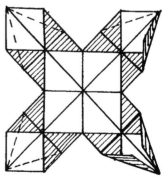

6

Goldfoil eight-pointed star

❖ *Double sided gold/coloured foil*
  scissors
  glue
  (ruler)

Measure and cut a square of foil.

1 Fold the square in half diagonally, open out, and repeat with the opposite corners, then open the foil once again.

2 Fold the square in half.

3 And again in half.

4 If a centre star is wanted, fold in half once more, and cut a V shape at the tip. For a four-pointed star simply cut the tip off. Open out the last fold. Cut a square off as shown — the square does not need to be accurately measured.

5 Open out the foil and cut 4 slits.

6 Fold each point at the tip and glue together.

Variations can be made by gluing the stars back to back or on top of each other in various combinations.

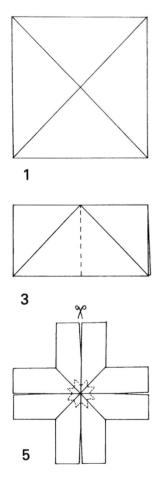

1

2

3

4

5

6

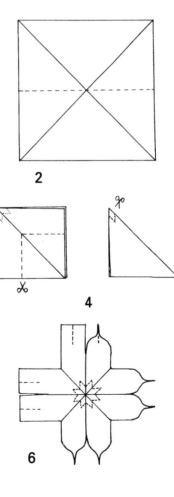

Goldfoil round star

❖ *double sided gold/coloured foil*
round objects (jar lids, cups etc.)
pencil
scissors
glue

Place the round object on the foil and draw around it. Cut the circle out.
1 Fold the circle in half.
2 And again in half.
3 And once more.
4 Open out the circle, and draw a small inner circle (free hand). Cut along the creases to the inner circle.
5 Using a pencil, place the tip midway between the cuts and roll the foil around the tip from either side. Remove the pencil and gently glue the top flap down. Stars of different sizes can be glued together in various combinations. Three stars within each other can also make a festive candle holder.

Woven hearts

❖ *2 strips of paper (glazed wrapping paper*
or painted paper) in contrasting
colours (the length should be approximately 3 times as long as the width)
1 narrow strip of paper for the handle
scissors
glue

1 Fold 2 strips in half.
2 Place one an top of the other with folded edge at the bottom. Hold them firmly together and cut the top corners round to form an arc. Make 2 cuts as shown. The cuts should be slightly longer then the width of the folded paper. This can be measured by holding the 2 pieces at right-angles to each other.
3 Weave the separate halves of the heart together as shown:
A between 1, around 2, between 3
B around 1, between 2, around 3
C between 1, around 2, between 3

4 Glue the handle to the inside of the heart.

Vary the width and number of the cuts to produce different designs. If the heart is to be hung on a branch, the handle should be quite long.

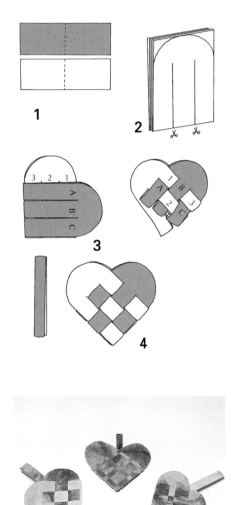

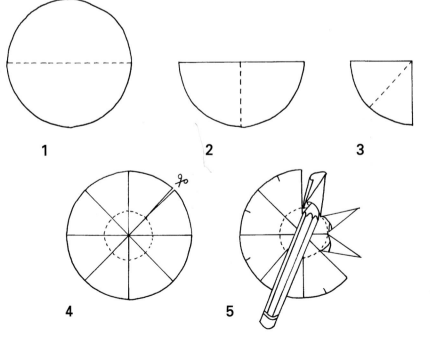

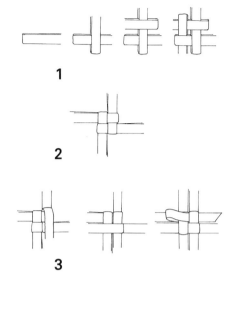

1

2

3

4

5

6

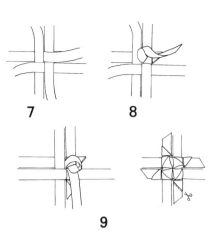

7

8

9

Woven star

❖ *4 identical strips of double-sided painted paper (longer than A4)*
or strips of (fairly wide) gift wrap ribbon
scissors

Fold each strip in half and trim the ends to a half point.

1 Interlock the strips.

2 Tighten the weave.

3 Secure the centre weave by a second interlock.

4 Fold the first point of the star.

5 Slip the pointed end of the strip under the lower right-hand loop and pull tight.

6 Rotate the star and repeat for the other 3 points on that side. For the

final point, the loose strip from the previous point will have to be lifted to slip the end under the loop.

7 Lift all four top strips up towards the centre and fold them down on the opposite side. This will hide the points.

8 The centre points are woven by curling a strip and then slipping the end into the gap shown.

9 Push the end in until it comes through the bottom right-hand point. It can then be pulled gently tight. While pulling with the right hand, support and guide the curl with the left.

Finally, rotate the star and repeat for the other 3 centre points. Trim the 4 strips where they extend beyond the points. The top side is now complete.

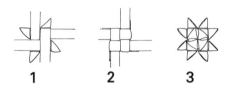

1

2

3

To finish:

1 Turn the star over.

2 Open out the strips to expose the weave underneath. Then weave them together as in stage 3.

3 Follow previous stages 4 to 10° to complete the star.

Glitter glue can be added to the star if desired.

Geometric thread decorations (Chinese good luck eye)

Although these may look complex, they are great fun to make and are easily managed by children as young as six.

❖ *strip of thick paper (approx length 10 times the width)*
cotton yarn/embroidery thread, in various colours
gold/silver yarn
glue
scissors
thread to hang
(sequins)

1 Fold the strip of paper as shown. After the first three folds, open the strip out, then continue to fold. Thereafter open the strip out every two folds, and continue. Note: the creases should not join each other exactly towards the end.
2 Fold *A* to *B*.
3 Push *C* inward to create a space.
4 Enclose the space by bringing *D* to corner *C,* and *E* to corner *F.*
5 Continue to wrap the strip around the geometric shape. Cut and excess paper off the end of the strip and glue the final flap down.

6 Choose a colour of yarn. Apply glue to one face and stick the yarn down. Wind the yarn around the shape as shown. Be careful not to crush the form, but ensure the yarn is pulled firmly. The first round of yarn should always cross from one face to another in the middle of the crease.

When the yarn has reached the first face again, continue to wind it around the form, following the first round on the *inside,* When changing the colour of the yarn, always stop and start in the same area (first face). Do not worry about that part looking messy, as it will be covered up with the upper weave.
7 When the lower half is nearly filled with yarn, push pins into the corners (the pins may need to be coated with glue) to prevent the yarn from slipping off. If you wish the under weave to remain visible, stop winding the yarn just short of the corners and start filling the upper half by following the first round on the *outside.* Again it is effective to let some of the under weave show, so do not cover it completely at the end.

The decoration can be hung either from one of the points, or from the midpoint of an edge.

Stick sequins on if desired.

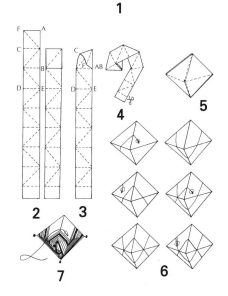

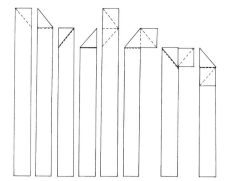

The story of Saint Nicholas

Long ago, longer then we can remember, Bishop Nicholas lived in a city called Myra in Asia Minor, which is now Turkey. Myra was a beautiful city with a large harbour. Many merchants lived there and every day ships came from all the countries around the Mediterranean Sea. Around the city many farmers grew grain and vegetables, which they sold at the market and in the port. Bishop Nicholas was good to all people and would help anyone in need.

Once a merchant of Myra had three daughters. His wife had died and he was so saddened by her death that he no longer took care of his business affairs. And so he became very poor. When his three daughters were old enough to get married there was no money to give them a dowry. He did not know what to do, because without a dowry none of his daughters would ever get married.

It was early spring. The trees were blossoming and the people of Myra looked very happy. In his distress the merchant had an idea: if he sold one of his daughters into slavery he would have enough money for the dowry of the other two.

When Bishop Nicholas heard of this talk about town, he took his purse and, in the middle of the night, went as quietly as he could to the merchants house. There he threw a purse with money through the open window and ran away.

The next morning the merchant found the money in the purse and thought a miracle had happened. He praised God for this wonder. Now his oldest daughter could marry, and so it came about.

But now no money was left for his second daughter to get married. Again Bishop Nicholas heard of this and came in the middle of the night and threw a purse through the open window. When the Merchant found this purse he was very happy indeed, for his second daughter could marry.

Now, when the time came for the third daughter to be married, the merchant wanted to know who was making such a generous gift to him and his family. So he hid himself. One night he saw a man with a big cloak throw a purse through his open window, and he caught hold of the man's coat as he ran off, but the merchant did not see his face.

The next morning he asked the people of Myra whose coat he had and they recognized it and told him it was the Bishop's. Then the merchant was afraid, for he realized how selfishly he had behaved. He went to the bishop and fell on his knees and vowed to become a better man.

There are many more stories about Bishop Nicholas. Sailors told the stories in all the ports they visited. After his death people all over Europe started to revere Nicholas. In 1087 his relics were brought to the city of Bari in southern Italy, which in those days was part of the Spanish Empire.

There are few saints whose miracles are depicted as often as his. In the Cathedral of Winchester there is a baptismal font on which are carved some of his legends. There, and in many other places he is shown with the wings of an angel.

In Russian Orthodox churches merciful Nicholas (as he is called there) is depicted on the iconostasis.

In Prague on December 6, you may see the bishop walking through the streets accompanied by two others: a little black devil and an angel.

Dutch and German immigrants brought his festival to North America. There he became Santa Claus, riding in a reindeer-sleigh.

In Holland and in Flanders the festival of Saint Nicholas is still celebrated on a grand scale. It is told that every year at the end of November the Bishop comes by ship from Spain. Until the celebration of his festival he rides a white horse over the roofs of the houses. On the evening of December 5 he comes to each house and gives everyone a present. In his big golden book are written all good and bad deeds of the people who promise to do better next year.

Another story is told of Bishop Nicholas. One year summer came without any rain. The earth became parched and barren. When it was harvest time there was nothing to take home, for all plants had died. So the people of Myra did not have much to eat. There was no corn to bake bread, and people began to starve. They had sold all their belongings for food but nothing was left. The whole country was stricken by famine. No ship entered the harbour any more, because there was no longer anything to sell.

Then one day a storm-damaged ship needing repairs sailed into harbour. The ship lay deep in the water and the people of Myra wondered what the ship was carrying. They asked the captain who told them that his vessel was full of grain. Here was a miracle: Here was the food they needed!

But the captain would not give or sell them any of his cargo of grain. He said: "This grain is for the Emperor in Constantinople. Every sack of grain is counted and if just one is missing, I will be imprisoned for life. I cannot give you any of this grain, I have to consider my own life."

The people wept and begged, and then turned angry. They wanted to climb aboard the ship and steal the sacks of grain. But the captain and the crew took up arms and kept the people of Myra at bay.

But some people went to Bishop Nicholas and told him what had happened. So the Bishop went to the harbour came and greeted the captain.

"Why don't you give some of your grain to my people? Don't you see how hungry they are? Do you want us all to die?"

The captain repeated what he had said to the bishop. "I cannot give you any of my grain, because I will be imprisoned if anything is missing."

Then Bishop Nicholas asked him: "Would you give us any of your grain, if I could show you that there will be no sacks missing?"

The captain laughed and told the bishop that is was impossible for anyone to make the grain multiply. But when he looked into the bishop's face he saw such a kindness, that he said: "You may show me what you mean. You may unload sacks of grain from my ship as long as the sacks in the ship do not get less. I can see very clearly whether the cargo lightens, because the ship will lie higher in the water. So you may show me what

you can do. But if the ship rises by only one finger, all the grain must be returned."

"It is not me who can do such a thing," Bishop Nicholas said. Then he asked ten men, standing on the shore to come and unload some of the grain. They came on board and unloaded one sack after another onto the quay, while the captain and his crew hung over the rail and looked carefully to see whether the ship would rise. But no matter how carefully they looked, while ten strong men carried sacks of grain ashore, the ship did not rise in the water. And when the captain looked into the hold of his ship he was even more surprised, for not one sack was missing!

Then Bishop Nicholas told the men to stop, for he

saw there was enough grain to feed all the people of Myra until the next harvest.

The next day the captain sailed out of the harbour of Myra and wherever he came, he told everyone about the miracle that had happened to his grain.

Among sailors there was yet another story of Nicholas, for they all knew of the time when Nicholas had sailed on a ship during a storm. The bishop had taken care of the ship and it reached the next harbour safely.

One November, when storms sweep over the Mediterranean Sea and the surrounding land, some sailors had been at sea for many days while the weather turned increasingly foul. Looking out to sea, they noticed a sudden lull in the wind which left them in complete silence. They all knew what that meant: a violent storm was brewing. On the far horizon they could see a little black cloud which dame nearer and nearer. They hurried up the mast to reef the sails. But far quicker than they expected, the storm came over them, and one of the sailors lost his hold and fell to the deck where he lay lifeless.

The storm beat the ship furiously and the sailors feared for their lives. Suddenly one of them remembered the miracles of Bishop Nicholas, and called to him in distress: "O Bishop Nicholas, come and save us!"

At that very moment a man stood next to him saying: "You called me. Here I am."

And he stretched out his hand over the water and immediately the storm stopped. Then he went to the sailor lying on the deck, touched him, and he stood up as if nothing had happened.

St Nicholas festival

On December 6 the festival of St Nicholas is celebrated. Children can leave a shoe or boot by the window the evening before. In the morning they will be greatly excited to find something inside from St Nicholas. This can be a tangerine, some nuts and raisins and some biscuits (obviously not ones they have baked themselves), wrapped together in a napkin and tide with a ribbon. It is also exciting for the child to receive a simple rhyme in their shoe from St Nicholas, commenting on the progress and changes over the last year of their life.

Here is an example:

Here I am once again
Writing with my golden pen.
Great changes have I seen this year
Too many to write about, I fear.
Beautiful drawings you've learnt to do
And your writing's come on too.
It gives me greatest joy to see
How helpful you can sometimes be.
I see too that you've grown quite tall
Your smile brings pleasure to one and all.
I bid you now a fond farewell
What next year brings — who can tell?
Your loving friend
St Nick

The letter should always be positive, but when the child gets older — especially in the preteens, St Nicholas can also comment on one or two aspects that could be improved — this is always taken in good faith from St Nick.

... But dear oh dear, it grieves me sore
How you argue more and more ...

Scandinavian peppercakes

These delicious cookies make a tasty alternative to ginger bread, and are ideal for decorating with royal icing.

❖ *285 g (10 oz) golden syrup (corn syrup cannot be substituted)*
 285 g (10 oz) sugar
 285 g (10 oz) butter
 2 eggs
 2 level tablespoons ground cloves
 2 level teaspoons bicarbonate of soda/baking soda
 830 g (1 lb 12 oz) plain flour.

Heat sugar, syrup and butter in a large saucepan. Stir the mixture gently until sugar has dissolved. Remove the pan

from the heat and stir in the cloves. Allow the mixture to cool for 15 minutes. Add 2 or 3 tablespoons of the flour to the mixture and stir in well. Dissolve the bicarbonate of soda/baking soda in $^1/_4$ cup of warm water, then add it to the saucepan. Add the eggs. Gradually stir in remaining flour. The last of the flour may need to be kneaded in. Transfer the dough to a large bowl and cover with a tea-towel. Leave dough for 24 hours at room temperature before baking.

Set the oven at Gas Mark 5 (190°C, 375°F). Using plain flour, roll out dough until very thin. Cookies should be placed on baking paper or oiled trays. Bake in the oven for about 10 minutes, or until golden brown.

Decorating the peppercakes

❖ *1 egg white*
Icing sugar/powdered sugar (sifted)

Add icing sugar/powdered sugar to the egg white until the mixture is thick and slowly falls off the spoon, this is important as runny icing will be very difficult to control. Attach a fine nozzle to an icing bag/piping syringe, and fill with the mixture. Try it out on a paper or napkin. Best results are achieved holding the nozzle 2 to 3 cm (1 in) above the biscuit where it is easier to direct the flow of icing. A fine nozzle will block from time to time with tiny lumps of icing sugar, so it is useful to have a clean pin or needle on hand to unblock it. Any royal icing sugar not immediately needed can be kept at the right consistency by placing a damp cloth over the bowl. If the icing has become too stiff, a very small amount of water can be added.

Deluxe truffles

These rich truffles make an excellent Christmas gift.

We Are Shepherds

M Wilson

We are shep-herds and we sing of__ lots of jol-ly things, we can dance and we can shout, we can wave our__ caps a - bout. The__ stars shine a - bove us, the snow shines be - low and__ we are so hap-py in this wond'-rous glow.

❖ *180 g (6 oz) quality plain chocolate*
100 g (3$^1/_2$ oz) icing sugar/powdered sugar
2 tablespoons crème fraiche
$^1/_4$ cup of cocoa powder
2 egg yokes
100 g (3$^1/_2$ oz) soft butter
2 tablespoons of rum or brandy

Gently melt chocolate in a double boiler. Beat egg yokes with sugar until thick and creamy. When chocolate has melted, add butter and crème fraiche, mixing well. Add the chocolate mixture to the egg mixture and stir in the brandy/rum. Transfer the mixture to a lunch box and chill until it is firm enough to roll into balls (about 1 hour in the freezer, 8 hours in the fridge). Put the cocoa powder on a plate, and roll the truffles in the cocoa to give them a fine coating. Chill for a further hour in the freezer — or longer in the fridge, and then store them in an air-tight container in a cool place until needed. Makes approximately 35 truffles.

For making the box, see p.24

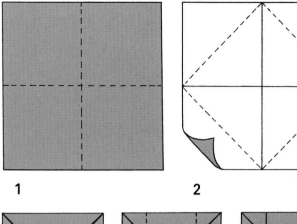

1   **2**

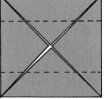

3   **4**   **5**

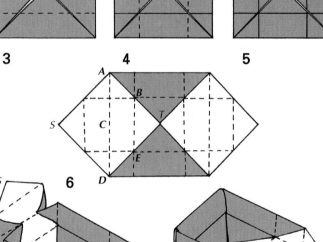

6

7   **8**

9   **0**

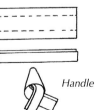

Handle

Origami boxes

❖ *2 squares of paper (wrapping paper or painted paper)*
small paper rectangle, or sprig of sprayed holly (for handle)
scissors
glue

1 Place square down, coloured side facing up, and fold in half from top to bottom and from side to side, opening the square in between.
2 Turn paper over (white side facing up) and fold corners into the centre.
3 Fold top and bottom edges into the centre and open out again.
4 Fold side edges into the centre and open out again.
5 Open out the sides.
6 Placing a finger underneath crease *AB* push it forward so that *A* meets *C*. Repeat for crease *DE,* where *D* meets *C.*
7 Fold in point *S* to meet the other points at *T.*
8 Repeat steps 6 and 7 for the fourth side of the box.
9 Completed base.
0 For the lid, repeat steps 1 to 8 with the other square, but in steps 3 and 4 fold the top and bottom, and the sides slightly short of the middle as shown. This will ensure the lid fits over the base.

   For paper handle, fold the edges of the rectangle towards the middle, and glue down. Twist the strip into a loop and trim the overlapping edges with scissors. Glue the handle onto the lid of the box.

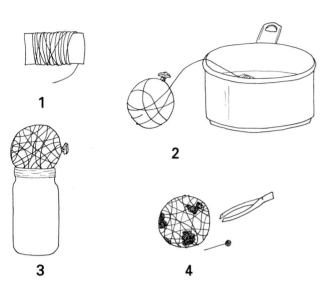

String balls (thread balloons)

These are very simple to make, but a little messy. It is therefore worth making several at the same time.

❖ *small water balloons*
   small piece of cardboard
   white thin cotton yarn (about 8 metres long)
   milk pan
   2 tablespoons of plain flour
   tweezers
   thread for hanging
   gold/silver spray

1 Wind the yarn around the piece of cardboard.
2 Blow the balloon up and tie it.

Make a glue by putting the plain flour in the milk pan and mixing in 1 cup of cold water. Bring to the boil, stirring constantly. Remove from the heat and allow to cool a little. Immerse the thread in the glue.

Wind the yarn around the balloon. While winding, run the yarn between thumb and forefinger to remove excess glue. If the balloon is a little oval, try to push it into shape by winding the yarn tighter around the poles than the equator. All areas of the balloon should be covered fairly equally (avoiding the knot).

3 Place the balloon on a glass jar to dry for 24 hours or more. The ball should become brittle and hard.
4 Using a pin, pierce the balloon in several places. The balloon should shrink away from the sides, leaving a hollow string ball. If the balloon pulls the thread inward, it has not dried enough.

Remove the bits of balloon with tweezers, then loop a fine thread around one of the yarns for hanging.

Spray the ball with silver or gold.

Straw stars

❖ *straws of natural colour*
   A sharp knife
   Pointed scissors
   A basin of water
   An iron

Soak the straws in water for about an hour. Cut down into the tops a little way with a sharp knife and iron them open further with a hot iron. You can also leave the wet straws uncut and iron them flat straight away.

Both the cut-open and the ironed straws can be made into very wide or into very narrow strips (cut with a ruler and a sharp knife). Straw stars made of cut-open straws have the disadvantage that they have a good side and a less good side, so that they look best against a background.

Straw stars made from straws which have not been cut open are the same

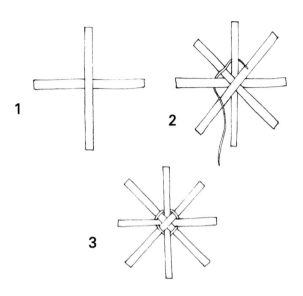

on both sides, and so are more suitable for mobiles, for use on the Christmas tree or to be hung in front of a window.

In the examples given in this book gold thread is always used for suspending the stars; but any other colour can be used, for instance, red.

Cut the straws into two or three lengths depending on the size of the star.

Eight-pointed star

1 Lay four straws of equal length crosswise upon each other.
2 Put your forefinger on the point where the straws cross each other to hold them in place and weave a thread round the straws taking it first over the topmost straw, then under the next, then over the one after that, and so on.

3 Finally tie the two ends of the thread together behind the star.

Alternatively, you could lay the straws crosswise on a block of wood and pin them down so that both hands are free to bind the straws together.
4 Cut the points of the stars to a particular shape.

Sixteen-pointed star

Make two eight-pointed stars (as above) and lay one on top of the other. Bind the stars together with a thread in the same way as described above. The thread of one of the eight pointed stars can be cut away. In the photogaph above you can clearly see the binding thread of the eight-pointed star, and the second outside thread of the sixteen-pointed star.

With more practice you can make this star by laying all the straws for a sixteen-pointed star on top of each other at the same time, working the thread through them all and tying it up. Altering the length and width of the straws will vary the result. Stars with a greater number of points can be made. By alternating wide and narrow, short and long, flat and hollow straws you can make innumerable varieties.

A straw ball

❖ *straws*
  a sharp knife
  glue
  a gold thread

Iron the straws flat and cut them into strips about 3 mm (¹⁄₈ in) wide. The ball consists of eight rings. Because the rings are all stuck over each other the diameter of the innermost ring must be a fraction smaller than that of the next one and so on.

1 As the difference is scarcely perceptible the best way is to stick the two ends of the innermost ring with slightly more overlap than those of the next.

2 Make the first two rings, allow them to dry fully and then stick them together in the form of a cross making sure that the joints of the straws do not coincide exactly. The glue of these rings stuck together must now dry fully because this is the foundation for the rest.

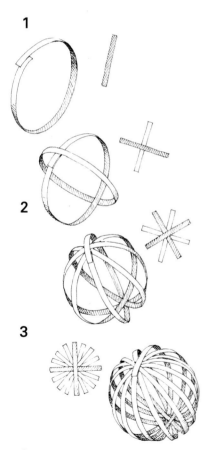

1

2

3

4

3 Make the remaining six rings and allow them to dry too. Then fill up the gaps between the cross in the following way: begin by sticking two rings in the middle between the cross. Once this is quite dry stick the remaining four rings in the intervening spaces.

Allow the glue to dry properly, then glue a piece of thread on to one of the rings.

To avoid damage in storage place an extra ring at right angles round the other rings to keep the tension.

Sprayed greenery cards

❖ *silver spray*
spraymount
cuttings of greenery such as cypress or fern
dark card

Flatten the cutting of greenery in a flower press or between books. This may take a couple of days. Place the greenery face down on some newspaper and apply spraymount. Carefully place the greenery face up on the dark card and arrange the leaves as desired. Press down firmly.

Apply silver spray and leave to dry. This is very important (if the leaf is removed before the spray has fully dried the silver will smudge). The silver leaf can then be stuck on to another card.

Greenery can also look effective on a silvery-white card with a little glitter added to the "branches."

Potato printing

❖ *3–4 large potatoes*
small cookie cutters
sharp knife with smooth blade
water-colour paints
2–3 paint brushes
white or pale coloured paper

For potato print Christmas cards:
❖ *coloured cardstock*
gold/silver pens
glitter glue
paper glue

Scrub the potatoes and cut in half, ensuring the cut surface is smooth and

flat. Push the cookie cutter well into the flat surface, and cut round the shape with the cutter still in place. Remove the cutter. The cut shape should stand out about $1/2$ cm ($1/4$ in) from the potato. Free-hand shapes can of course also be cut out. Prepare as many potatoes as desired. The paints can either be transferred to a plate, so the potato is easily dipped into it, or the paint can be applied direct to the potato with a brush. Print onto the paper, applying fresh coats of paint as necessary. Prints look particularly effective if their are different shades in a colour.

When the prints have dried, cut them up as desired for cards and stick the cut piece onto appropriate coloured card. The print pattern can be enhanced by outlining some of the shapes with gold or silver pen and adding a little glitter glue. "Framing" the print with gold or silver pen, and adding a sticky star can also be effective.

Painted paper

Painting simple colour tones on paper is great fun for children and the end results can be put to all sorts of uses such as Christmas cards, gift tags, en-

velopes, woven hearts, woven stars and Nativity sets?

❖ *paper. The type of paper used is fairly important. Many drawing papers do not hold water colours well. A4 (Letter size) photocopying paper is suitable for collages, envelopes and Nativity sets. A3 (Double letter) similar paper is good for woven stars. Children find a thicker paper (such as wallpaper lining) easier to handle when making woven hearts.*
set of watercolours
large paintbrush
2 or 3 sponges

In general it is best to choose one theme colour per paper. Take a sponge and soak it in water. Gently wet the entire sheet of paper. Then, using the other sponge or paintbrush, apply colour.

Always start from a light shade and work towards a dark shade. If the sheet is to be basically green, start by covering the entire sheet with a lemon yellow, then add areas of dark yellow, light greens, dark greens and finish with prussian blue. The colours will merge and flow to from a lovely variety of tones. If double-sided painted paper is required, ensure the one side is completely dry before applying paint to the reverse side.

When painting with children, always remind them to be gentle with the brush/sponge on the paper, otherwise the paper will start to shred. Varying tones can also be splashed and dabbed on. Make sure the brush/sponges are washed out well between colours. For paper kings (see page 46), the red, blue and green sheets can be spattered with a bit of gold or silver. When the paintings have dried out completely, they can be flattened in a book, weighed down by a pile of books on top. Leave the paintings to flatten for 24 hours.

Collage cards

❖ *thin paper*
   painted paper in various colours (it is best to use thin paper such as photocopying paper)
   scissors
   glue
   folded card to mount the picture on

When making up a scene, always work from the background to the foreground. For example: start with the sky, then work towards the foreground. Leave details such as trees

and figures to the last. Keep figures simple.

It is easiest to start with the head and neck, then a simple triangle for a tunic, an arm, a cape and a hat.

It is best to choose contrasting tones of colour within the piece of painted paper, rather than building up too many layers, making a thick and clumsy card.

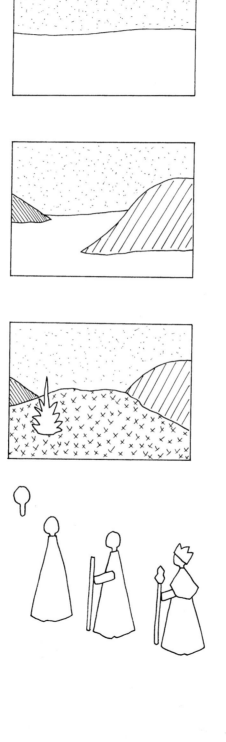

29

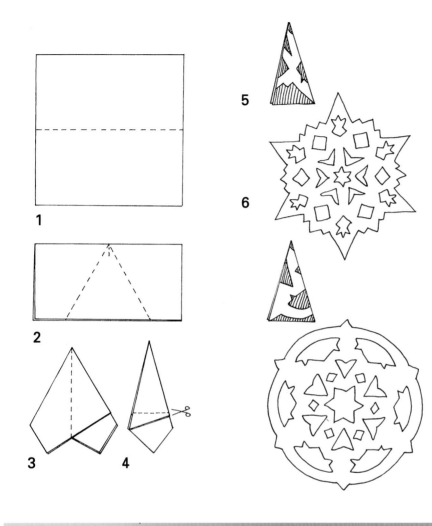

Christmas snowflake

❖ *silver paper*
small, sharp scissors
glue
dark card for mounting
silver pen

1 Cut the silver paper into squares approximately 8 cm (3 in) wide. Fold the paper in half.
2 Gently fold in half again to mark the centre, then open out.
3 Fold the half into thirds (children may need help with this).
4 Fold in half once more, and then trim.
5 Cut small pieces out from either side (never cut right through from one side to the other, except for at the very tip which will form the centre).
6 Open up the folds and flatten.

For smaller children it is easier if a simple design is pencilled on for them to follow, otherwise they will easily cut through the snow flake and land up disappointed with the results. Older children can of course have fun making up their own designs. See above for some cutting suggestions.

Depending on the silver paper used, the snowflakes may need to be flattened between books overnight. This will make it easier to glue on to the dark card.

On the reverse side of the snowflake, apply small amounts of glue on the six points and also some a little nearer the centre (spraymount can also be used). When the snowflake is glued down, the design can be enhanced by carefully adding some silver dots and lines.

Double-sided goldfoil cards

❖ *double sided gold/coloured foil*
 small, sharp scissors
 glue or spraymount
 dark or white cardstock for mounting

It is worth practising designs with
scrap paper first. This will also help to
decide on the desired size.

1 Cut a square. Fold the paper in half.
2 Fold in half again.
3 Fold diagonally.
4 Trim the edges as shown.
5 Cut a simple pattern as shown.
6 Carefully unfold the square.
7 Flaps pointing outward should be
folded down, and flaps pointing inward folded up to reveal the under-
colour.
8 A folded square can also be cut into
two to form a frame separate from the
inner design.
9 The frame, too can be cut up to
form corner decorations. Flatten the
final design before gluing it to the
cardstock.

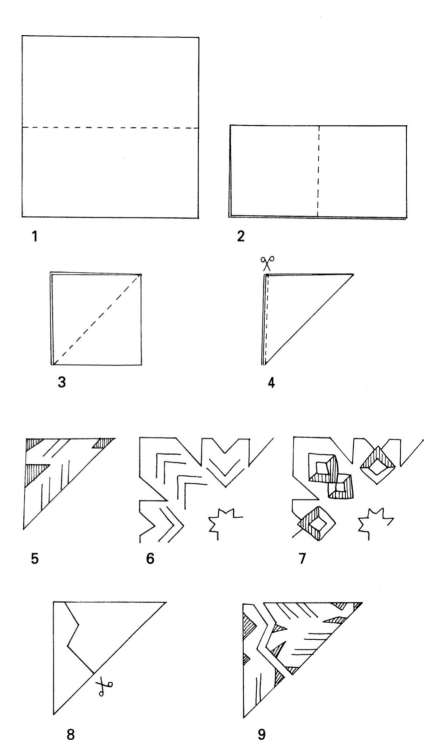

Thread Christmas cards

❖ *tracing paper*
thick paper or cardstock
needle and gold/silver thread (approximately twice as thick as standard sewing thread)
round headed pin or compass
sticky tape

Trace the dots of the required pattern. Place the tracing paper on top of the thick paper and hold carefully in place or stick down with Blutack. Taking the pin or compass end, firmly poke through each dot so the pattern will transfer to the thick paper beneath.

Remove the tracing paper, checking first that no dots have been missed. Reverse the paper.

Thread the needle. Using tape, stick the end of the thread down on to the paper at the side of the pattern. Poke the needle through the first hole to the right side.

Follow the individual pattern instructions. Always ensure the thread is pulled just tight enough to avoid baggy loops, but not so tight that the card warps.

End by taping down the thread on the reverse side.

Snowflake

This is the simplest design and can be managed by fairly young children. On the reverse side, the thread should never move more that one dot to the side.

A–B, (B–1), 1–2, (2–3), 3–4, ... 13–14, (14–B), B–C, (C–15) and repeat as for first diamond, then work round until all the diamonds are complete.

Star within a circle

It is important with this design that the holes marked with letters are slightly bigger than the other holes around the circumference. This will act as a guide and prevent mistakes occurring.

A–1, (1–2), 2–3, (3–4), 4–5, ... 10–11, (11–12), 12–13, ... 20–21, (21–22), 22–B, (B–C), C–23, (23–24) and repeat as for the first section. The sections can be sewn in this order: A–B, C–D, E–F, B–C, D–E, F–A.

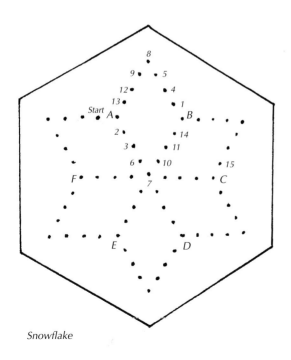

Snowflake

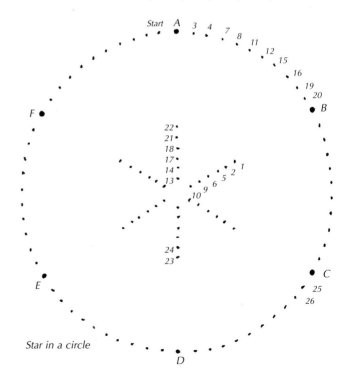

Star in a circle

Angel

It is particularly important with this design that the thread tension is even or the card will easily bend.

For head and dress
1–A, (A–B), B–1, (1–2), 2–B, (B–A), A–2, (2–3), 3–A, (A–B), B–3, (3–4), 4–B ... until compete.

For wings
14–C, (C–D), D–14, (14–15), 15–D, (D–C), C–15, (15–16), 16–C, (C–D), D–16, (16–17), 17–D ... until wings are complete.

Six-pointed silver star

This is a fine design which can be effectively done with sewing thread of normal thickness.

1–A, (A–B), B–1, (1–2), 2–B, (B–A), A–2, (2–3), 3–A, (A–B), B–3, (3–4), 4–B, (B–A), A–4, (4–5), 5–A, (A–B), B–5, (5–6), 6–B, (B–A), A–6, (6–1), 1–C, (C–D), D–7, (7–8), 8–D, (D–C), C–2, (2–3), 3–C, (C–D), D–9 ... C–6, (6–13), 13–C, (C–D), D–14 ... continue as for first section.

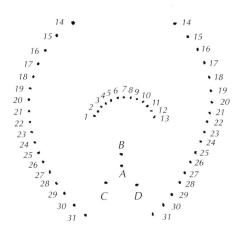

Angel

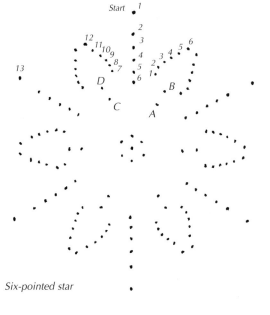

Six-pointed star

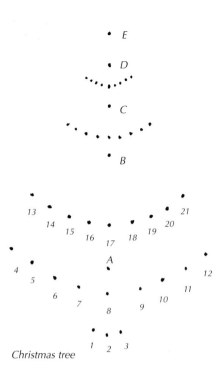

• E

• D

• • • • • • • •

• C

• • • • • • •

• B

13   21
14   20
15   19
16   17   18

A

4   12
5   11
6   10
7   8   9

1   2   3

Christmas tree

Christmas tree

This design can be sewn up in any way. This is one suggestion:

A–1, (1–2), 2–A, (A–B), B–4, (4–5), 5–B, (B–A), A–3, (3–6), 6–B, (B–C), C–13, (13–14), 14–C, (C–B), B–7, (7–8), 8–B, (B–C), C–15, (15–16), 16–C, (C–B), B–9, (9–10), 10–B,

(B–C), C–17, (17–18) ... continue until tree is complete. Then stitch together the ends of the branches to form a curve on each section.

Small beads can also be added to decorate the tree.

Trim the card as desired and mount the design on to another coloured card to hide the reverse-side stitching.

Envelopes and gift tags

Envelopes

❖ *painted paper*
envelope (new and opened out)
glue
gum arabic (available from art shops)

1 Place envelope face down on *back* of painted paper, and draw round the envelope with a pencil.

Remove the envelope and cut out the pencilled shape.
2 Place the envelope on the paper exactly as before and holding it firmly in place, fold the paper with the envelope inward to form the necessary creases.

Remove the envelope and glue the paper as the envelope was glued

Paint the flap rim with gum arabic and allow to dry.

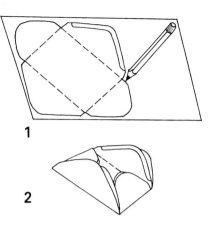

1

2

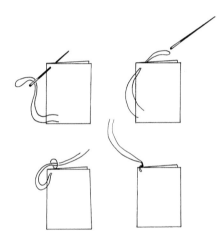

Gift tags
❖ *coloured cardstock*
  painted paper
  glue
  glitter glue
  silver/gold stars
  silver/gold pens to decorate

Cut the cardstock to size and fold in half. Decorate as desired. To thread the tag follow diagram.

Transparencies

❖ *tracing paper*
  cardstock (dark colour)
  precision penknife (or stanley knife)
  glue (pritt or Uhu)
  tissue paper or transparency paper

Trace transparency pattern. Cut out appropriate size of cardstock (see individual patterns for measurements.)

Measure off 7 cm (3 in) on either side for wings and gently score with a knife to ensure neat fold back.

Transfer design from tracing paper to cardstock, pressing hard with a sharp pencil. Place cardstock on newspaper or cardboard and cut along pencil indentations with a sharp knife. Then remove unwanted cardstock.

Turn cardstock to reverse side. Place appropriate coloured tissue paper over cut holes and mark around the edges with a pencil, ensuring the colour does not overlap to another hole.

Cut tissue paper along marked lines.

Glue tissue paper around edges or glue cardstock, whichever is simpler, and carefully stick tissue down onto cardstock.

Hold the transparency up to the light to make sure the tissue has covered the hole completely, and is not overlapped anywhere.

A double layer of tissue paper gives a richer colour. Also different coloured tissue papers together give greater variety of tones.

Cardstock can be trimmed and shaped along top edge.

Measurements and further instructions (in order of difficulty):

Angel with baby
❖ *cardstock: 32 × 26 cm (13 × 10$\frac{1}{2}$ in)*
Transfer Mary, Star and Angel separately, positioning them as desired.

Shepherds and crib
❖ *cardstock: 26 × 16 cm (10$\frac{1}{2}$ × 6$\frac{1}{2}$ in)*
Transfer ox, ass and window in right hand corner of cardstock first, then transfer the remaining design ensuring star is placed top centre.

35

Angel with baby

Shepherds and crib

Angels

Angels
❖ *cardstock: 32 × 16 cm (13 × 6^1/$_2$ in)*

Kings
❖ *Cardstock: 32 × 19 cm (13 × 7^1/$_2$ in)*

Christmas Tree
❖ *Cardstock: 38 × 22 cm (15 × 9 in)*
Transfer and cut out tree and figures 1, 2, 3, 4, 5 and 8 first. Using traced pattern, line up figure 6 next to figure 5, transfer and cut out. Then lastly, line up figure 7, transfer and cut out.

Kings

Wax nativity set

❖ *modelling wax in appropriate colours
2 smooth faced water bottles.*

Fill the water bottles with hot water (not too hot) and place the wax between them. After five minutes the wax should be soft enough to mould with ease.

1 For kings and Mary, work the wax into a very thin, flat approximate square. If the wax hardens, return it between the hot water bottles.

2 Shape the square into a tunic, pulling the arms forward. When the wax is very thin it easily forms graceful folds.

3 Taking slightly more wax for the cloak than the tunic, work it also into a thin square. Arrange it with folds in an approximate semi circle and join it to the tunic, leaving the body hollow.

Extra wax can be worked for stoles.

4 The head should be given a long neck to fit in between the cloak and the tunic to help balance the head.

Joseph can be made by shaping the thin, flat wax into a cone and then adding a cowl.

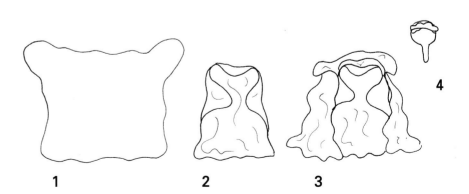

1 **2** **3** **4**

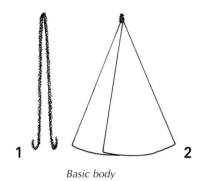

Basic body

Paper nativity set

❖ *1 pipe-cleaner*
  1 bead (or equivalent made from e.g. wax/Daz/Fimo); 1.5 cm ($\frac{1}{2}$–$\frac{3}{4}$ in) diameter with a hole through the middle.
  tracing paper
  scissors
  glue (Uhu recommended)
  double-sided painted paper (see p. 28) in appropriate colours
  twig (for Joseph)
  toothpick/cocktail stick (for Shepherd's crook)

Using the diagrams, trace required clothing. Cut round tracings to make pattern pieces.

Choose contrasting colour tones on painted paper for different items of clothing and place pattern pieces appropriately.

Draw round the pattern pieces and cut out the clothes. Using the pointed end of a scissor blade, poke through any places marked with an *X*.

Start each figure by making a basic body.

Basic body

1 Fold pipe-cleaner in half and turn up bottoms by $\frac{1}{2}$ cm ($\frac{1}{4}$ in).
2 Take the tunic (see p. 47), glue the shaded area, and then form a cone around the pipe-cleaner, leaving the folded tip of pipe-cleaner sticking out.

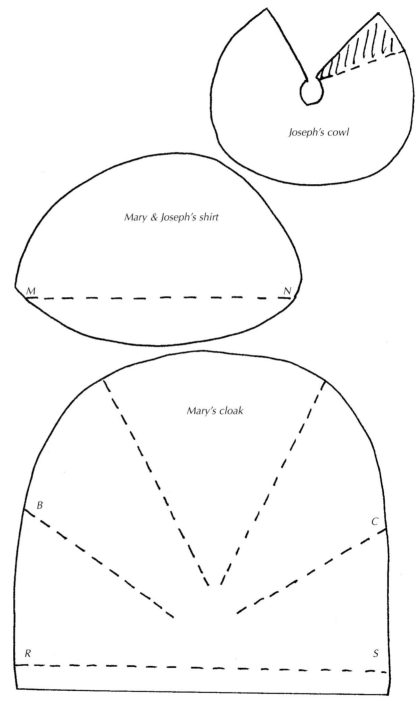

Joseph's cowl

Mary & Joseph's shirt

Mary's cloak

Mary / Joseph

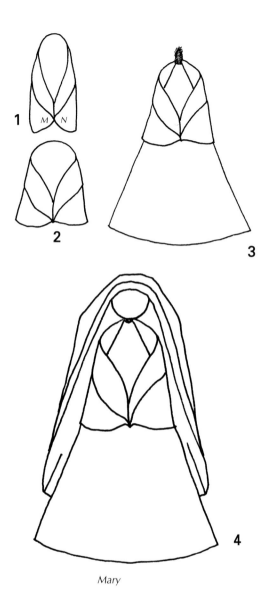

Mary

Joseph

Mary

1 Fold Mary's shirt (page 43) along dotted line. Glue *M* and *N* together to form hands.

2 Push hands back and squeeze paper at shoulders.

3 Place shirt over basic body.

Fold Mary's cloak along dotted line *R–S*. Mountain fold along remaining dotted lines to form folds in cloak.

Gently bend cloak in half and glue *B* to *R,* and *C* to *S* (over existing fold).

4 Glue bead on to pipe-cleaner. Glue cloak to head, and to tunic at the back, or as desired.

Joseph

1 Fold Joseph's shirt (page 43) along dotted line. Taking basic body, wrap shirt around tunic and glue left hand approximately to centre front of tunic, leaving right hand free.

2 Apply glue to shaded area of Joseph's cowl, and glue down slightly squint. Slip cowl over pipe-cleaner.

3 Glue bead onto pipe-cleaner. Glue hat (on Shepherds' pattern) down onto bead and crumple hat as desired. Glue thin twig to right hand.

Right wing

Angel's crown

Left wing

Collar

J

K

Angel's hair

Angel's cape

P

P

P

Angel

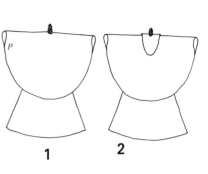

1

2

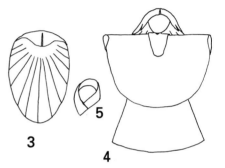

3

5

4

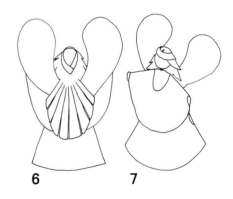

6

7

Angel

1 Bend Angel's cape gently in half along dotted line and push over pipe-cleaner on to basic body. Glue sleeves together at points P.

2 Push collar over pipe-cleaner and fold back.

3 Taking angels hair, cut along every marked line. Apply glue to shaded area and lift flaps J and K and glue down so they meet in the centre to form a parting.

4 Glue bead onto pipe-cleaner. Glue and stick down hair onto bead.

5 Glue angel's crown to form a V-shape, and glue over hair.

6 Glue shaded area of wings and fold along dotted line. Slip wing through hair and stick down to cape at back.

7 Wings can then gently be folded backwards.

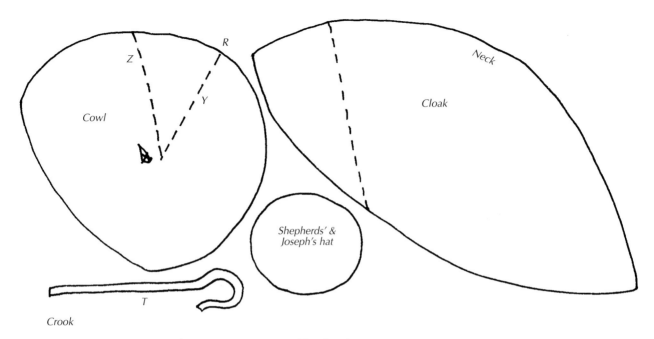

Cowl

Z

R

Y

Neck

Cloak

Shepherds' & Joseph's hat

Crook

T

Shepherds

Shepherd

1 Taking shepherd's cloak and fold along dotted line. Wrap cloak around basic body and glue to tunic at approximately chest level, so cloak hangs free at hem.

2 Taking shepherd's cowl, mountain fold along dotted line *Y*, and valley fold along dotted line *Z*.

3 Push cowl over pipe-cleaner and position with point *R* exactly in front.

4 Glue bead to pipe-cleaner. glue hat over bead and crumple/fold as desired. Taking cocktail stick, apply glue at one end and wind length *T* of shepherd's crook around glued end of cocktail stick. Shepherd's crook can be glued to body at either point *R* or point *S*.

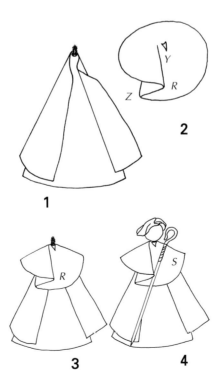

King

1 Taking king's shirt, fold upwards along dotted line to form a crease, and then open up again. Push the shirt over spipe-cleaner on basic body.

Form hands by joining points *A* and *B* under shirt front.

2 Glue shirt front down at point *C* and fold hands *A* and *B* up, to enable them to carry gift.

3 Taking king's cloak, fold downwards along dotted line and push cloak over pipe-cleaner. Glue the cloak to the tunic along hemline.

4 Taking collar, push over pipe-cleaner making sure the larger side is at the back to form a high, stand-up collar.

5 Glue on bead. Taking crown, glue shaded area and stick down. Glue crown to head. Crown should sit well down and back.

6 Taking a small piece of appropriate coloured paper, fold/crumple into any desired shape to represent a gift. Glue gift to hands.

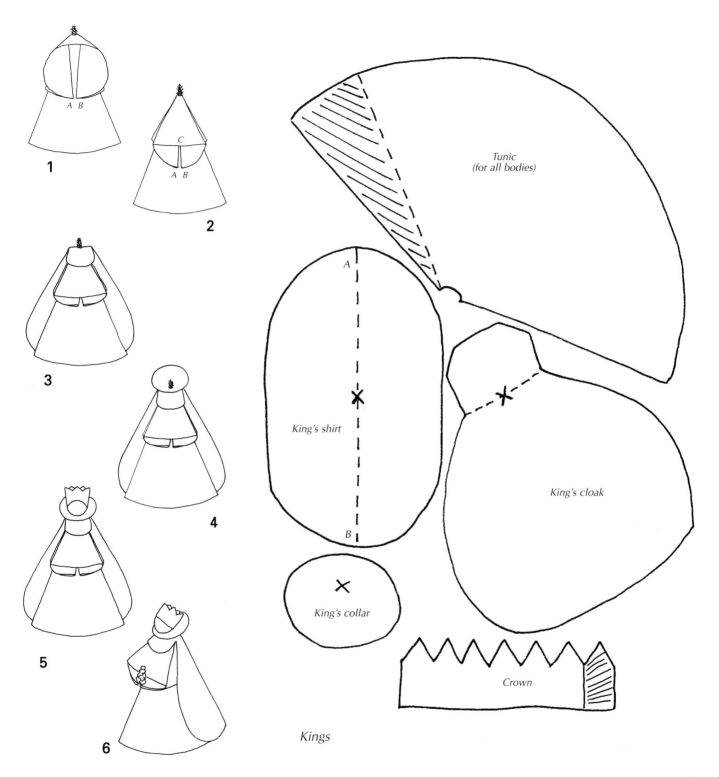

1

2

3

4

5

6

*Tunic
(for all bodies)*

A

King's shirt

B

King's cloak

King's collar

Crown

Kings

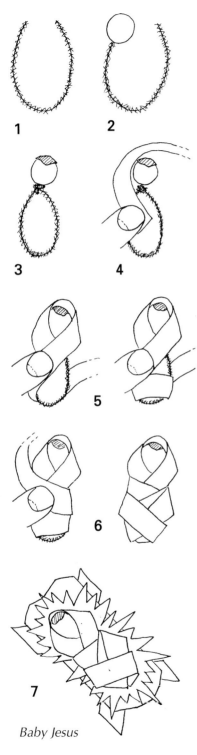

1   2

3   4

5

6

7

Baby Jesus

Baby Jesus

❖ $^1/_2$ pipe-cleaner
  1 bead (or equivalent) 1 cm ($^1/_4$–$^1/_2$ in) diameter.
  1 strip of white/cream paper 21 × 1 cm (10$^1/_2$ × $^1/_2$ in)
  1 small circle of brown paper (for hair)

1 Bend pipe-cleaner into U-shape.
2 Glue bead onto one end.
3 Glue brown paper over hole in bead to make hair. Wind free end of pipe-cleaner around neck to secure in a loop.
4 Take strip of paper and hold one end to chest and wind around the head.
5 Keep winding paper until pipe-cleaner is completely covered.
6 Either glue end or tuck end in.
7 Lay baby in manger (see next).

Manger

❖ double-sided painted paper in
  — brown, 10 × 5 cm (4 × 2 in) rect-angle
  — pale yellow/straw, 6 × 4.5 cm (2$^1/_2$ × 2 in) oval

1 Take brown paper.
2 Fold brown paper in half.
3 Then in half again.
4 And once more.
5 Open out. There should be seven creases. Apply glue to one of the shaded areas.
6 Stick the other shaded area onto the glued surface.
7 Push down centre fold to form trough.
8 Fold manger in half and cut the legs and shape the trough as shown.
9 Legs should lie flat down on surface for stability.

For the straw:
1 Fold yellow oval in half.
2 Then into a quarter.
3 Cut jagged points around curved side (as shown). Open out and glue "straw" to inside of trough.
    Place baby on straw.

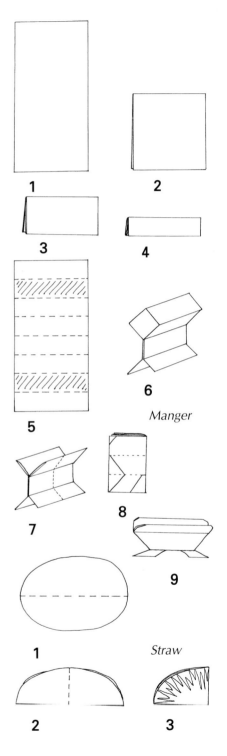

1   2

3   4

5

6

Manger

7   8

9

1

Straw

2   3

48

Paper nativity set and paper kings

Cloth nativity set

Basic body

❖ *2 pipe-cleaners*
  strip of flesh coloured stockinette (45 × 1.5 cm (18 × ¹/₂ in), stretching long-ways)
  fabric glue (Uhu) or needle and thread
  1 bead (or equivalent made from wax/ Daz/Fimo or similar), 1.5 cm (¹/₂ in) diameter, with a hole though the middle

1 Bend both pipe-cleaners in half.
2 Twist one around the other.
3 Bend the ends of the twisted pipe-cleaner back to the centre. This gives the basic proportions of a figure.
4 Taking stockinette strip, wind around the chest to secure the pipe-cleaners and then wind around the limbs, stretching the material a little as you wind.

Keep winding until body and limbs are completely covered, except for the feet, which should remain free so that shoes can be fitted if required.
5 Secure the end of the strip with glue or a couple of stitches.

Do not glue the bead on until the clothes have been fitted.

Shoes

❖ *Wax/Daz/Fimo*
  Cocktail stick/match

The shoe should be about 1 cm (¹/₂ in) long and about as wide as the end of a pencil.

Take enough wax (or equivalent) for two shoes. Divide into equal halves, and roll the piece into a ball.

Press the ball down on to a flat surface and elongate the shape. Using a fine stick poke a hole in one end in a horizontal direction. The hole should be big enough to fit the width of a pipe-cleaner.

When fitting the shoes on, turn the

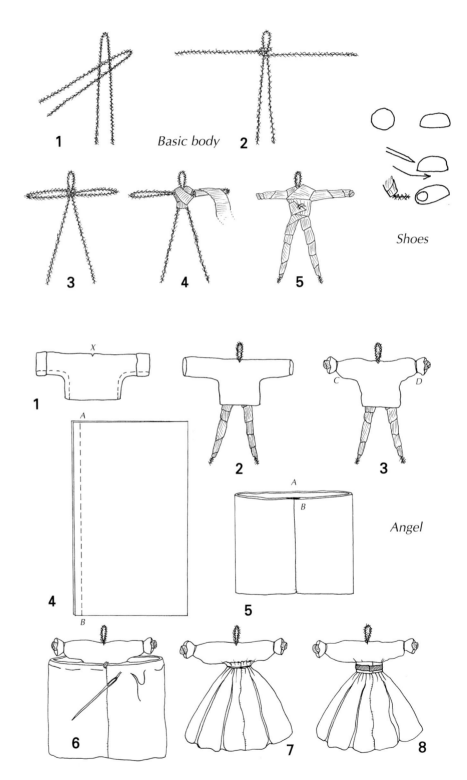

Basic body

Shoes

Angel

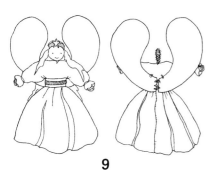

9

feet at right angles to the leg and glue the foot inside the hole.

To balance the figure, stick a small amount of Blutack, clay or plasticine (which should not be visible) to the base of the shoe.

Angel
Basic body
❖ *white/cream material (approx 30 × 15 cm, 12 × 6 in)*
white/cream ribbon for waist band, approx. 5 mm ($^1/_4$ in) wide
gold ribbon, approx. 2.5 mm ($^1/_8$ in) wide
white or golden wool for hair
needle and white thread
fabric glue (Uhu)
small gold star for head band

1 Using pattern pieces (page 52), cut out shirt, skirt and 4 wings. Taking angel's shirt, fold back wrists and then fold in half along dotted line. Sew together as shown.
2 Make a small hole at point *X*. Turn the shirt inside out. Taking the basic body, bend the arms up to allow the shirt to be slipped on. Push the neck through the hole and bend the arms back.
3 Push the sleeves up the arms until the hands are visible, then sew the sleeve to the wrists at points *C* and *D*, winding the thread around a few times to give a cuff.
4 Taking the angel's skirt, fold along dotted line and sew along line *A–B*.
5 Fold bottom half up and over top half to form a double skirt.
6 Sew the skirt to the shirt as shown, and then gather the waist by sewing large stitches around the top of the skirt and pulling the thread tight.
7 Finish off by winding the thread around the waist a few times.
8 Wind the white ribbon around the waist and glue at the back. Wind the gold ribbon over the white ribbon and glue at the back.
9 Taking two of the wing pieces, sew them together along the dotted line and then turn inside out. Repeat for the other wing. Tuck the free ends inside and sew the wings on to the back.

Glue the bead on to the neck, and glue the hair on to the bead. For the headband, measure the head with the gold ribbon, allowing an overlap for gluing. Glue the head band together before pushing it over the hair. Stick the small star centre front.

Drawing faces
Drawing a good face takes practice. Eyes are often drawn too high and too close together. The mouth is also often drawn too big.

The face of a doll can make or break its appearance, so it is worth practising first and then lightly doing the face in pencil before finally drawing it with a fine, black felt-tipped marker. Again, the pen should be tried out first on the surface — some pens run.

The eyes should be just below the mid line, and the mouth should form an equilateral triangle with the eyes (a mouth that is too high will give the appearance of a double chin.).

Eyebrows and nostrils can be added if desired, but should be done very lightly.

Mary
Basic body
❖ *red felt*
fine, blue cloth
red and blue thread and needle
thick red thread
brown wool
fabric glue

Using pattern piece No. 1 (p.53), cut out Mary's dress (red felt). Fold it in half along dotted line and make a small cut in the middle as shown.
1 Taking basic body, push the neck through the cut, and sew up the dress from hand to hem, right and left, making cuffs as shown.

Wrong

Correct

1

51

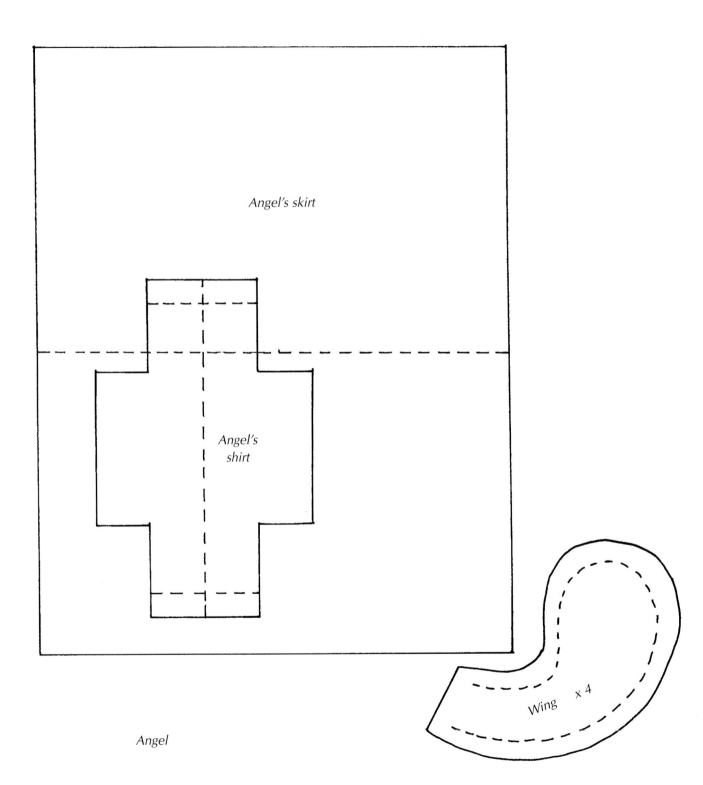

Angel's skirt

Angel's
shirt

Angel

Wing × 4

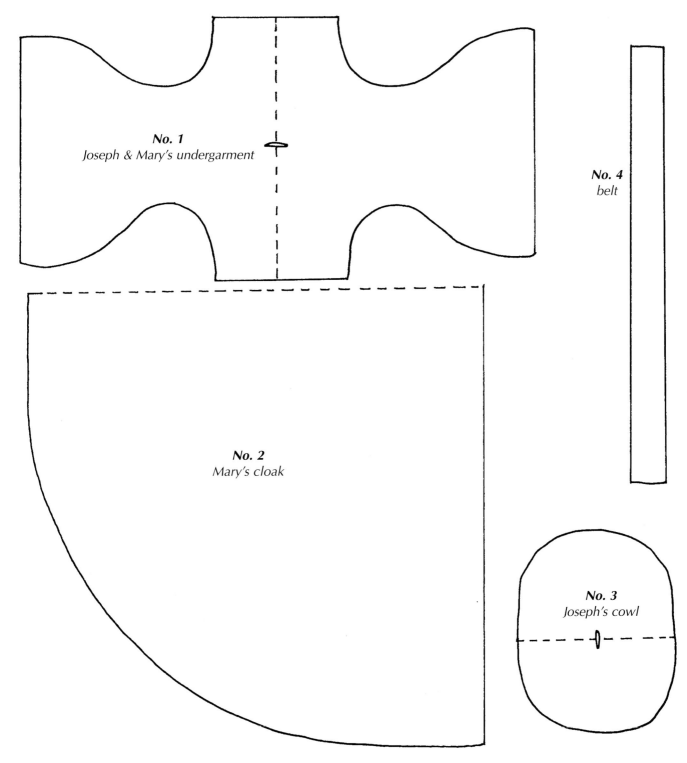

No. 1
Joseph & Mary's undergarment

No. 4
belt

No. 2
Mary's cloak

No. 3
Joseph's cowl

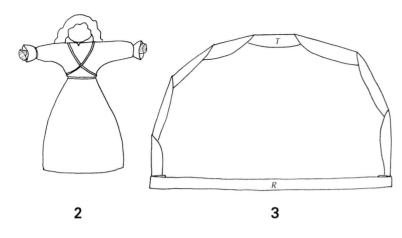

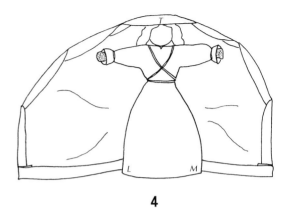

2

3

4

2 Taking some red thick thread, or a thin strip of red felt, wind around the chest to form a criss-cross and glue or stitch the ends at the back. Glue the bead onto the neck and glue on the hair. Turn the feet up so they are out of sight (no shoes are needed).

3 Cut out the Mary's cloak (blue cloth, pattern piece No. 2). Unfold the cloak and glue a hem around the edge as shown.

4 Glue the cloak to the head, at point *T* (hiding the hem) and to the bottom of the dress at the back, at point *R*.

5 Using blue thread, stitch the cloak to the sides of the dress at point *L* and *M,* and stitch around the neck of

the cloak (Gathering the cloth to form a hood). Make a number of folds and tucks as desired, stitching them firmly in place.

All the blue stitching can be done with a single thread — the needle can be pushed right through the figure.

Joseph
Basic body
❖ *brown felt*
   brown thread and needle
   white or grey wool
   glue
   twig
   shoes

Using pattern piece No. 1 (p.53), cut out Joseph's tunic (brown felt), and sew onto basic body as for Mary, but leave the wrists loose.

1 Cut out cowl (brown felt, pattern piece No. 3, p.53) and fold in half, making a small cut in the centre. Push the neck through the cut and glue or stitch down front and back, making a little fold.

Cut out belt (brown felt, pattern piece No. 4, p.53) and tie around the waist. Glue or stitch into position if it does not lie flat.

2 Glue bead onto neck and glue on hair and beard. Glue twig onto hand and glue on shoes (see p.50).

5

1

2

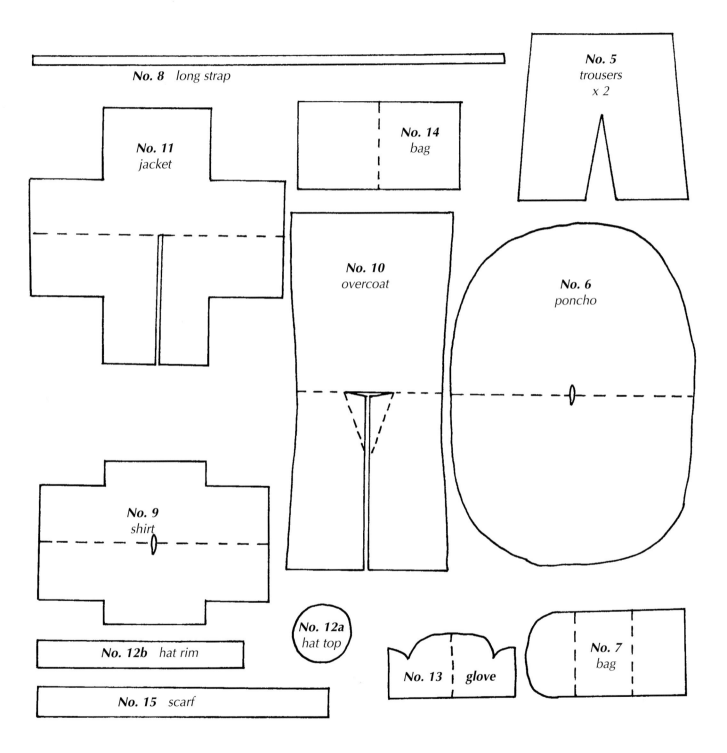

No. 8 long strap

No. 5 trousers x 2

No. 11 jacket

No. 14 bag

No. 10 overcoat

No. 6 poncho

No. 9 shirt

No. 12a hat top

No. 12b hat rim

No. 13 glove

No. 7 bag

No. 15 scarf

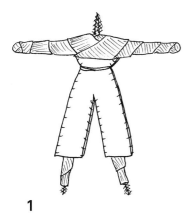

1

Shepherds

❖ *3 basic bodies*
  4 or 5 different coloured felts in browns,
    greens and greys
  3 cocktail sticks
  thin cardboard
  appropriate threads and needle
  thick red thread
  glue
  3 pairs of shoes
  white and brown wool

1 Using three different coloured felts, cut out two trouser sides in each colour (pattern piece No. 5, p.55). Taking a basic body, put the two pieces front and back with the waist just under the armpit, and sew the pieces together, finishing off by winding the thread around the waist a few times.

Repeat for the other two bodies.

Shepherd No. 1

Cut out shepherd's shirt and overcoat (pattern pieces Nos. 9 and 10, p.55 — contrasting colours). Fold the shirt in half and make a small cut for the neck.

1 Taking basic body with trousers, fit the shirt on and sew up the sides.

Fit the overcoat over the shirt. Fold back the lapels and stitch or glue them down.

2 Cut out belt (pattern piece No. 4, p.53) and tie it around the waist securing the overcoat.

Shepherd No. 2

Cut out shepherd's poncho (pattern piece No. 6 — contrasting colour to trousers). Fold in half and make a small cut for the neck. Taking the basic body with trousers, fit the poncho on and stitch up the sides.

Cut out the bag (pattern piece No. 7), fold along the dotted lines and stitch up the sides, leaving the flap loose.

3 Cut out strap for bag (pattern piece No. 8). Overlap and glue the ends together forming a circle. Glue the strap to the bag under the flap, and fit the bag over the shepherd's shoulder.

Shepherd No. 3

Cut out shepherd's jacket (pattern piece No. 11, p.55). Taking basic body with trousers, fit the jacket on and sew up the sides first.

4 Then taking some white wool, place it in a line from chin to chest and fit the jacket over it. Stitch up the front, leaving the white wool a little exposed.

Finish the shepherds off as follows:

5 Cut out 3 hats in different colours (pattern piece Nos. 12a and 12b, p.55). Sew the two pieces together as shown.

Glue the beads onto the necks of the shepherds, and then the hair, followed by the hats.

6 Cut out 3 pairs of gloves (pattern piece No. 13, p.55 — contrasting colours). Fold the glove over the hand with the thumb uppermost. Sew the gloves onto the hands and finish off by winding the thread around the wrists to secure the glove.

7 Cut out the bag for shepherd No. 3 (pattern piece No. 14, pp.51, 53). Stitch up the sides and stuff with

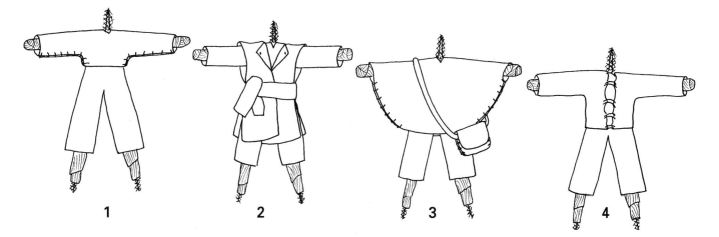

1   **2**   **3**   **4**

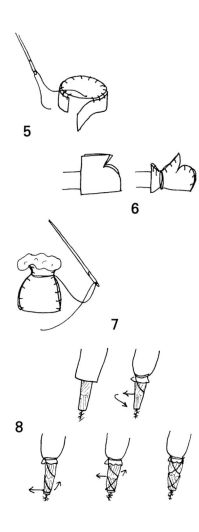

5

6

7

8

white wool. Wind the thread around the neck of the bag leaving some of the white wool exposed.

Use the same thread to make a strap around the shepherd's body, stitching it onto the waist at the opposite side.

Cut out scarf for shepherd No. 2 (pattern piece No. 15), and tie around the shepherd's neck.

8 Taking the thick red thread, sew on criss-cross leggings. Glue on shoes.

9 Finally, using the thin cardboard, cut out 3 hooks to glue on to the cocktail sticks for shepherds crooks. After they have been glued on, thread can be wound around if desired.

Sheep

❖ *2 black/brown pipe-cleaners*
white/grey/brown wool
needle and thread (thread colour should match the wool colour)

1 Taking one of the pipe-cleaners, form a small loop in the centre.

2 Form the horns by bending the pipe-cleaner as shown.

3 Bend and twist the pipe-cleaner ends back at point *C*, so that *A* and *B* meet at the tail.

4 Bend the tail down at point *D*, and tuck the sharp ends in.

5 Cut the second pipe-cleaner in to

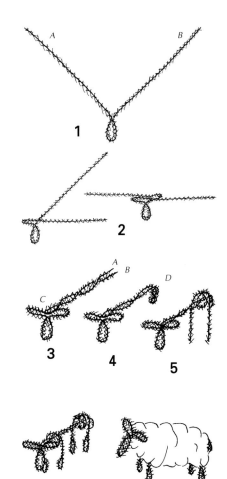

1

2

3 **4** **5**

6 **7**

two halves. Taking a half twist it around the back bone just in front of the tail to form two back legs.

6 Turn the sharp ends up to shorten the legs. Repeat for front legs.

7 Taking the wool, tease it in to a long strip and wind it around the neck, body and tail, making the body the fattest part. Using a needle and thread secure and shape the fleece as desired, the stitches should be small and invisible.

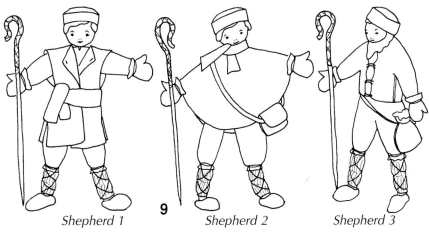

Shepherd 1   **9**   *Shepherd 2*   *Shepherd 3*

Baby Jesus

❖ $^1/_2$ pipe-cleaner
  1 bead (or equivalent) 1 cm ($^1/_2$ in) in diameter
  white/cream, cotton ribbon approx 21 × 1 cm ($8^1/_2$ × $^1/_2$ in)

Follow instructions for Baby Jesus, Paper Nativity Set (p.48). No hair is required as cloth is more flexible and can be stretched to cover hole.

Manger

❖ some thin twigs (6 cm, $2^1/_2$ in long)
  dried grass
  glue
  dark thread

1 Select two of the thickest twigs and cut them in half. Tie the halves together to form two crosses.
2 Select the next thickest twig for the base of the trough. Apply glue at points A and B and carefully but firmly stick down the cross twig; this may need to be held in position until the glue is dry.
3 Apply glue to the rising sides of the trough and place the branches crossways to complete the trough.
4 When the glue has dried, the structure should be stable and hardy. Apply glue to the inside of the trough, and sprinkle over with the dried grass.
  Glue, or simply place the baby within.

Setting for cloth nativity

❖ Shoe box with lid
  Strong scissors
  Dark blue paper (for lining base)
  Dark blue cloth
  Sharp, long needle and dark thread
  Glue

1 Cut away shaded area on shoe box and lid.
2 Glue section A to the left hand corner of the shoe box, and line the base with the dark paper (a paper surface is ideal for balancing and sticking the figures down).
3 Glue B and C together to form a small platform for the angel to stand on. Place the platform upside down on a square of dark paper. Measure the sides and cut away the shaded area as shown.
  Fold the dark paper over the sides and glue down to the inside.
  Drape the blue cloth around the shoe box to measure the required amount (allow for a hem, and take care to stretch the cloth right around the perimeter — it is easy to cut it too small.) Cut the cloth to size.

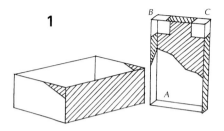

1

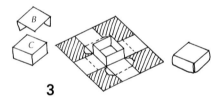

2

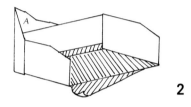

3

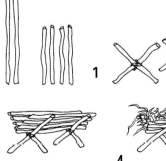

1

2

3   4

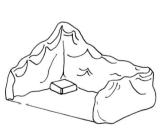

4

5

4 Apply glue all around the sides of the shoe box at the base (inside and out). Fold a hem in the cloth and stick the fabric on to the cardboard.

This will leave a lot of loose, excess cloth around the top edge which can be arranged in folds with pins pushed through the cardboard. When the cloth is arranged as desired, it can be sewn into place and the pins removed.

5 Place the platform in the left-hand corner.

Trees can be added to the setting by cutting small twigs of greenery and sticking them into a plasticine/Blutack base.

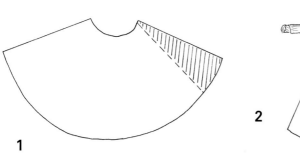

1

2

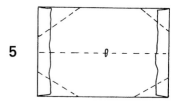

5

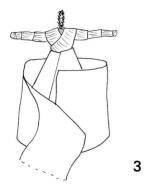

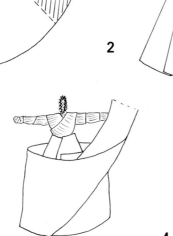

3

4

6

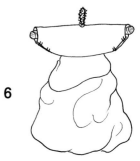

7

8

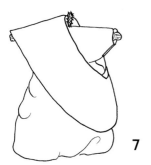

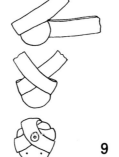

9

Kings

❖ *3 basic bodies*
  3 paper cones (see pattern)
  satin ribbon in red, blue and green (ap-
    proximately 5 cm wide and 63 cm
    long,)
  fabric glue
  needle and appropriate threads
  selection of small beads (or equivalent)
    to represent gifts
  white wool (for blue king's beard)
  small gold and silver beads
  sequins

Cut the ribbon into strips as follows:
  robe 27 cm (11 in)
  shirt 9 cm (3¾ in)
  stole 17 cm (6¾ in)
  turban 10 cm (4 in)

1 Cut out 3 paper cones and apply glue to the shaded area.

2 Wrap the cones around the basic bodies and stick down.

3 Thread the needle with the appropriate thread to match the satin ribbon being used. Apply glue to the cone and stick robe down, starting from the base and winding up to the waist. Make sure the ribbon overlaps the base of the cone, so no paper is visible.

4 As you approach the waist, fold and shape the ribbon around the cone and tuck in the end. Taking needle and thread, secure the ribbon by stitching the folds and joins where required, to make the desired style. The stitching can go right though the paper and also through the body.

5 Taking the shirt ribbon, apply glue to shaded area. Fold over and stick down.

6 Fold the shirt in half and make a small cut in the middle for the neck. Push the neck through the hole. Fold in and stitch the shirt sleeves to make a tight wrist.

7 The stole can either be placed over one shoulder, or if a small cut is made in the middle (for the neck) placed over both shoulders.

8 The stole can be gathered, hemmed and stitched in many different ways. Sew (or glue) on beads and sequins as desired. Push arms down and forward to enable the king to carry a gift.

9 Taking the head, push it onto a spare pipe-cleaner, stick or needle, to make it easier to work with. Narrow the turban ribbon to about 3 cm (1 in) and then glue the strip in half to form a narrow band. When gluing the turban to the head, make sure the frayed edge of the ribbon is innermost.

The turban can be styled in many different ways with the ends tucked in, but a number of stitches will be needed to secure it in place. Glue on a sequin and bead centre front.

When making the blue king, glue the beard on before the turban. Draw the face and then remove the bead from the pipe-cleaner and stick onto the figure.

Apply glue to the hands and carefully place gift between them, using pressure until the glue has dried.

Christmas Eve

Christmas Eve can have its own special exciting atmosphere.

It can work well to leave the decorating of the tree until that day, so when the children come to spend the evening around the tree, the impact is greater and there is a feeling of Christmas having really started. The nativity set is in place — but the Christ Child is absent. He will be born during the night, and the children will look for him before breakfast on Christmas Day.

The evening can start with a candle-lit supper. The family then gathers around the tree to hear the story from the Bible (Luke 2:1–20). For small children this can be difficult to follow, so it helps if they have a series of relevant pictures to feast their eyes on. After the Bible story, carols can be sung — everyone can choose their favourite.

Children particularly like rhythm and order in a festival — a routine that they can become familiar with and look forward to every year.

Floral candle holders

❖ *block of oasis*
 plant pot base (saucer or jar lid can also be used)
 long candle
 variety of evergreen
 gold spray (optional)
 variety of flowers and/or berries
 clippers

If gold is wanted in the display, spray selected cuttings of evergreen leaves and allow to dry. Cut the oasis block to the desired size (approx. 9 cm, $3^3/_4$ in square is easy to work with). Trim the corners so that it will fit easily into the base. Soak the block in water for 10–15 minutes, then place on base.

Trim the base of the candle so that it is thinner than the widest point, then push the candle down about 4 cm ($1^1/_2$ in) into the centre of the oasis block.

Trim the stems of the flowers and foliage as necessary. When pushing in the cuttings, it is best to start at the base, working round and then upwards.

Do not pack the display too full — more can always to added later. Try to arrange the display symmetrically. Do not add the big flowers, such as roses, until most of the gold/green foliage is in, otherwise they can end up hidden.

The oasis block should be watered daily, the display can then last through the twelve days of Christmas.

Goldfoil candleholder No. 1

❖ *square (approximately 13 cm, 5 in) of double-sided foil*
 scissors
 glue

1 Fold the square in half from top to bottom and from side to side, opening out after each fold.
2 Turn the foil over and rotate round. Fold the diamond in half from top to bottom and from side to side, opening out after each fold.
3 Fold all four corners to the centre and open out again.
4 Take the bottom corner and fold it up as shown, then open out again. Repeat with the other 3 corners to make a grid of creases.
5 With a finger nail, sharpen the creases of the inner square. Turn the foil over to the reverse side. With care, and using the existing creases, bring points *A, B, C* and *D* together by pushing the centre point inward.

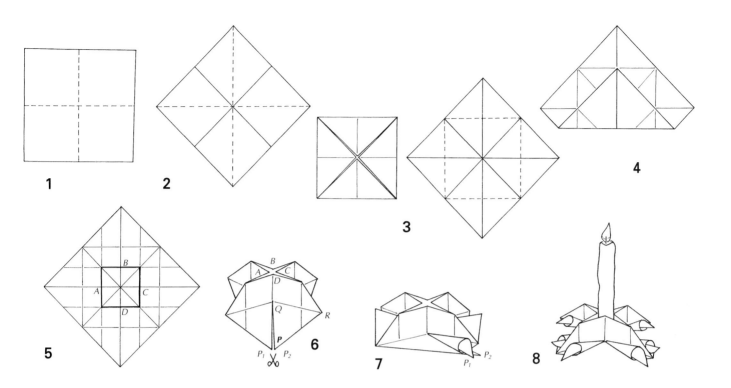

1 **2** **3** **4** **5** **6** **7** **8**

6 Cut along the line *PQ*. Repeat for the three remaining flaps. Now fold the eight cut flaps up along crease *QR* so they are at right-angles to the candle holder and form a steady base.

7 Roll the cut flaps and glue down as shown.

8 Open the centre out a little and place the candle in. The foil should then be pushed in and around the base of the candle to hold it firmly in place.

Candles

Never leave lit candles unattended. Make sure that goldfoil candleholders are not on wooden or plastic surface which may begin to smoulder when the candle gets low.

Take Heart, the Journey's Ended

French

Joseph

1 Take heart, the jour-ney's end-ed: I see the twink-ling
2 And how then shall we praise him? A-las, my heart is
3 Look yon-der, wife, look yon-der! An hos-tel-ry I

lights, Where we shall be be-friend-ed On
sore That we no gifts can raise him Who
see, Where tra-vel-lers that wan-der Will

Mary

this the night of nights. Now praise the Lord that
are so ve-ry poor. We have as much as
ve-ry wel-come be. The house is tall and

led us So safe un-to the town,___ Where
an-y That on the earth do live,___ Al-
state-ly, The door stands op-en thus;___ Yet,

men will feed and bed us, And I can lay me down.
though we have no pen-ny We have our-selves to give.
hus-band, I fear great-ly That inn is not for us.

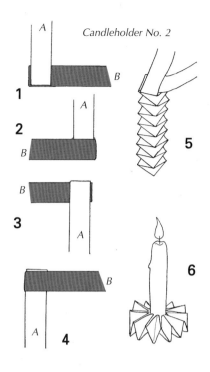

1

2

3

4

Candleholder No. 2

5

6

Goldfoil candleholder No. 2

❖ *2 strips of double-sided foil (for a small holder both can measure 1.5 × 35–40 cm, $^1/_2$ × 14–16 in; for a larger holder one can be 2.5 × 145 cm, 1 × 58 in; the other 4 × 80 cm, $1^1/_2$ × 32 in. The strips can be made up of lengths of foil glued together.)*
  scissors
  glue

1 Glue the end of strip *A* to the end of strip *B*. Then fold *B* over *A*.
2 Fold *A* down over *B*.
3 Fold *B* back again over *A*.
4 Fold *A* up over *B*.

5 Continue folding in this way until the strips are finished. Glue the ends together.
6 Form a circle with the pleated strips by gluing the beginning to the end. Open the centre a little to let the candle in. A small piece of round paper can be glued to the base to stabilize the holder.

Goldfoil angel

❖ *white tissue-paper*
  teased sheep's wool
  goldfoil
  a blunt needle or fine knitting-needle
  glue

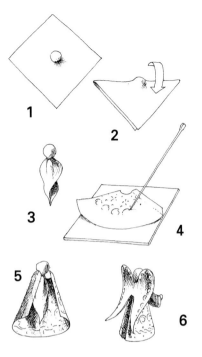

1

2

3

4

5

6

Goldfoil angel

A

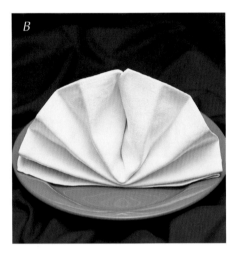

B

C

body, and the wings to the back. Take a little tuft of teased sheep's wool, spread this round the head for hair and glue it on. Finally make two little hands of tissue-paper and stick these to the arms.

Napkin folds

A Standing Christmas Tree
1 Using a folded paper napkin, start with the four free corners at the top left. Fold in half.
2 Hold the napkin down at point *X* and lift corner *A* to corner *B*.
3 Turn the napkin over.
4 Hold point *X* and lift corner *C* to corner *B*.
5 Press down folds firmly.
6 Lift napkin at point *X* and spread the four corners.

B Fan Napkin
1 Start with an open square cloth or paper napkin. Fold in half.
2 Accordion pleat just over half (seven folds works well).
3 Fold in half.
4 Fold back flap down.
5 Fold the end of the flap back and allow pleated sides to open out.

C Fleur-de-Lis
1 Start with an open square cloth napkin. Bring corner *A* to corner *B*.
2 Bring corner *C* and corner *D* to point *A*.
3 Bring corner *E* to point *F*
4 Bring *E* back up to point *G*
5 Hold napkin firmly, and turn over.
6 Bring right and left corners towards each other.
7 Tuck the right corner into the left.
8 Hold the tuck firmly and round out the base. Turn the napkin round.
9 Pull the top points outward.

1 Cut a square piece of tissue-paper 10 × 10 cm (4 × 4 in) for the head. Lay it on the table with one of the corners pointing away from you. Put a blob of wool the size of a big marble in the middle of the square.
2 Fold the paper over the blob so that the two opposite corners meet.
3 Shape it and tie off the head with a white thread.
4 Cut out the pieces for the body, arms and wings (page 65) by laying the goldfoil with the outside upper-most on a base that is not too hard, for example on a piece of soft card-board, and drawing the forms on the foil with a large blunt needle or a fine knitting-needle.
5 Attach the head by placing the neck inside the body and sticking the two edges of the body together to make a kind of funnel.
6 Stick the arms to both sides of the

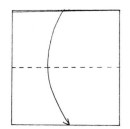

1

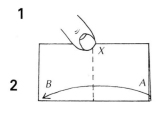

2

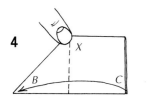

3

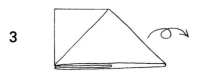

4

5

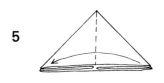

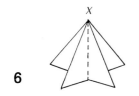

6

A *Standing Christmas Tree*

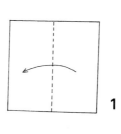

1

2

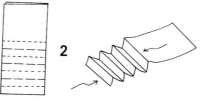

3

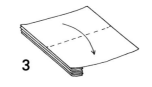

4

5

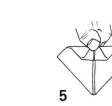

front view

B *Fan Napkin*

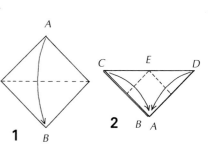

1

2

3

4

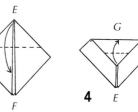

5

6

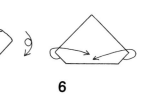

7

8

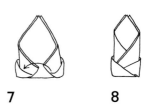

9

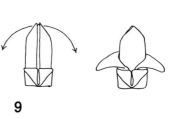

C *Fleur-de-Lis*

67

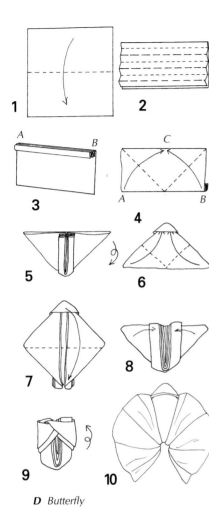

D Butterfly

D Butterfly

1 Start with an open square cloth napkin and fold in half.

2 Accordion-pleat the top half.

3 Holding the pleats firmly at point *A* and *B,* turn the napkin round.

4 Fold corners *A* and *B* to centre *C.*

5 Again holding the pleats firmly, turn the napkin over.

6 Tuck the outside corners into the triangular pocket.

7 Fold the napkin down just below the halfway mark.

8 Bring the side points towards each other and insert one inside the other.

9 Holding the tuck carefully, turn the napkin over and allow the wings to spread out.

Meringue ice-cream

This dish is best made on Christmas Eve, to be served with hot raspberry sauce after the Christmas meal the following day.

Meringues

❖ *3 egg whites*
170 g (5–6 oz) caster sugar
1 teaspoon natural vanilla essence
a pinch of salt

Beat the egg whites until frothy. Add the salt and continue to beat until the eggs can hold their shape. Add the caster sugar gradually, beating all the time. Finally add the vanilla essence.

Spoon the mixture in small dollops onto a tray covered with baking paper/baking parchment.

Bake on a low shelf at Gas Mark 1/4, (110°C, 225°F) for 2 hours.

Remove meringues from the oven, and turn them bottom side up on the tray. Using a skewer make a hole in the bottom of each meringue and then return them to the oven for half an hour to finish drying out.

Set aside about 6 of the meringues, and crush the rest.

Ice-cream

❖ *1 pint of double whipping cream*
  1 tablespoon natural vanilla essence
  110 g (4 oz) sugar
  a pinch of salt
  4 egg yokes, slightly beaten
  2 cups of milk

Whip the cream until thick. Stir in the vanilla essence and set aside.

Using the remaining ingredients make a custard as follows: Mix the sugar, salt and egg yokes. Heat the milk up and just as it starts to boil remove it from the heat and slowly add it to the egg mixture, stirring constantly.

Transfer the mixture to a double boiler and cook over a constant heat, (the water in the saucepan should be kept simmering). Stir occasionally, until the mixture thickens.

Add the custard to the cream and stir in gently.

Add the crushed meringues to the ice-cream, and transfer to the freezer for 1 to 2 hours. Remove, and mix the ice-cream well before transferring it to the serving dish.

Decorate the top with the whole meringues and return to the freezer.

Ice-cream may need to be removed from the freezer an hour before it is eaten.

Raspberry sauce.

❖ *450 g (1 lb) frozen raspberries*
  ¹/₂ cup of water
  ³/₄ cup sugar
  2 tablespoons lemon juice

Heat the water and sugar up in a pan until the sugar has dissolved. Add the raspberries and bring to the boil.

For a thin sauce remove immediately, for a thicker sauce, allow to boil for 5 minutes. Remove from heat and add the lemon juice.

Serve with the ice-cream while still hot.

Ding Dong! Merrily on High

Ding dong! mer - ri - ly on high in
Ding dong! ve - ri - ly the sky is

heav'n the bells are ring - ing:
riv'n with An - gels sing - ing.

Glo - - - - - - - - - -

- - - - - - ri - a, Ho -

san - na in ex - cel - sis!

2. E'en so here below, below,
   Let steeple bells be swungen,
   And *i-o, i-o-, i-o*
   By priest and people sungen.
   Gloria, Hosanna in excelsis!

3. Pray you, dutifully prime
   Your Matin chimes, ye ringers;
   May you beautifully rime
   Your Evetime Song, ye singers:
   Gloria, Hosanna in excelsis!

Hark the Herald Angel

Mendelsohn

Hark! the her - ald an - gels sing__ Glo - ry to the new born King,

Peace on earth, and mer - cy mild,__ God and sin - ners re - con - ciled.

Joy - ful, all ye na - tions rise,__ Join the tri - umph of the skies;__

With th' an - ge - lic host pro - claim, "Christ is__ born in Beth - le - hem."

Hark! the her - ald an - gels sing Glo - ry__ to the new - born King.

2. Christ, by highest heaven adored,
   Christ the everlasting Lord,
   Late in time behold him come,
   Offspring of the Virgin's womb,
   Veiled in flesh the Godhead see!
   Hail, the incarnate Deity!
   Pleased as Man with man to dwell
   Jesus, our Emmanuel.
   Hark! the herald angels sing
   Glory to the new-born King.

3. Hail, the heaven-born Prince of Peace!
   Hail, the Sun of Righteousness,
   Light and life to all he brings,
   Risen with healing in his wings.
   Mild he lays his glory by,
   Born that man no more may die,
   Born to raise the sons of earth,
   Born to give them second birth.
   Hark! the herald angels sing
   Glory to the new-born King.

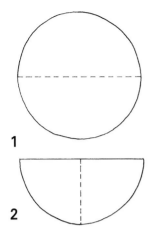

1

2

Tissue paper balls

❖ *14–20 circles of tissue paper in various*
   colours
   paper to make a small cone
   scissors,
   glue
   small circle of cardboard
   needle and thread

1 Take a circle and fold in half.
2 Fold in half once more.
3 Cut 2 curves partway as shown.
4 With the paper, cut a wide "skirt" and roll it into a cone. Secure the cone with glue.

5 Unfold the tissue circle and cut along the creases as far as the inner circle. Place the paper cone midway between the cuts. Wrap the tissue quatre around the cone and glue.
6 Repeat for the other 3 segments.
7 Repeat steps 1 to 6 for the other tissue circles. Thread half of these together followed by the small cardboard circle and then the remaining tissues. Tie the ends of the threads firmly together to form a tissue ball. Children will need help with this.

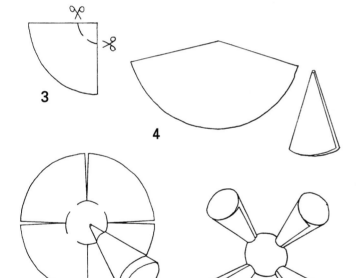

3

4

5

6

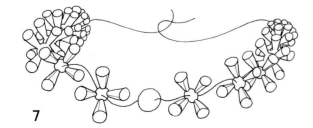

7

The Little Juggler

Adapted from an old French legend

Once upon a time many more than a hundred years ago, there lived a certain minstrel boy, a boy named Barnaby, whose tale I now will tell you even as it was told to me. He had neither mother nor father, no, not even a roof to call his own. He wandered far, to and fro, and in many places. Like a snail, he carried on his back all that he had in the world, for he owned only the clothes he wore and a few articles rolled inside a worn rug which he carried on his shoulders. These things inside his rug were his treasures: two sticks, a few hoops, some balls, and a handful of apples. For he was a street juggler, nothing more nor less.

Barnaby earned his bread by juggling and tumbling, dancing and singing. How to leap and spring, to juggle and balance objects in mid-air, these things he knew well, but nothing much besides. He knew nothing of books — in fact, he knew only what his father had taught him, for his father had been a juggler also.

Now, Barnaby's mother had died when he was a baby, but his father lived until the spring when Barnaby became ten. Until then they travelled the land together, amusing the people both high and low, in the market squares and at the fairs, at weddings and on feast days. For this the people tossed them coppers, and with these coins they bought their bread.

Now and again they had the good fortune to entertain the lords and ladies at some great feast within a castle. Then their pockets jingled with silver, and they sat gratefully in a dark corner of the great hall after they had finished their tricks, munching the leftover meat and pastries with the dogs.

After his father died, Barnaby was alone. In order to eat he did as he had been taught, for it was all that he knew. He spread his shabby rug in the squares on market day and leaped and danced and juggled with all his might.

He appeared at inns to entertain the guests. He even found his way across drawbridges and through strong gates of castles where he solemnly begged to be allowed to entertain the lord and his lady.

If the people laughed when first they saw the small clown, they ended by showering coins on his rug when his tricks were over, for Barnaby had been well taught indeed. Young as he was, all went well, or as best it could, the rest of that spring and through the months of summer as he trudged across the countryside. The sky was his roof and the weather and the people were kind to him.

But when the chill of winter began to creep into the houses and into the bones of men, fewer and fewer people stood still in the cold long enough to watch Barnaby at his tricks in the market place. In castles the lords and ladies wore their fur-lined mantles. In the monasteries the monks wore garments of lambs' wool as they prayed in their cold churches. In cottages the peasants put on all the clothes they owned.

And Barnaby, despite the exercise of tumbling and juggling shivered. The coppers he picked up were few indeed.

One day, frozen and forlorn, he stood on his mat and bowed. Snowflakes had started to fall. One person only watched the boy, a monk who had come to the market from a nearby abbey to buy provisions for the kitchen. When Barnaby had finished, the monk spoke to the boy, saying, "Where is your home?"

Barnaby looked at the ground and shook his head, saying nothing for fear that words would bring his tears.

"Come," said the monk, "come with me. You can warm yourself in our kitchen."

Barnaby did so. The abbey became his home.

But at first the little tumbler, for all the good fortune of having a roof over his head and decent clothes on his back and enough food to eat, moved among the monks sad and ashamed. He saw the monks about him, each serving God in his appointed way. Wherever he went, upstairs and down, in every quiet corner, in office and cloister, he saw the monks at work and prayer.

"Woe is me," he said. "O wretched me, what am I doing here? All the rest are serving God but me. I have no business here. I know not even how to pray aright and do naught but eat the bread they give me."

Barnaby grew yet sadder as Christmas approached, for all about him everyone worked harder still. On Christmas Eve in the little chapel the monks would present to the Christ Child and His Mother the things that

they had been making for them during the long year. One monk was writing a song. Another was penning the words to it. Still another was painstakingly copying a book of hours. Others were ornamenting its pages with flowers and scenes from the life of the Virgin Mary. Several monks together were carving a beautiful altar screen of oak for the little chapel that contained the statue of Our Lady and the Christ Child.

One day Barnaby knelt before the statue. "Holy Mary," he prayed, "how can I serve you?" Then in despair he wept. He hung his head and wished he had never been born. When he heard the bells ring for Mass, an idea entered his head. He sprang to his feet. "Shall I do it? Yes, I can and I will. I will do that which I have learned and thus, after mine own manner, I will serve the Christ Child and His Mother in her chapel. The others may honour them with songs and chants I will serve with tumbling."

While the monks filed into the great church for Mass, Barnaby ran and fetched his rug and his sticks, his hoops, his balls and his apples. Hurrying back to the little chapel, he removed his robe. He laid his shabby rug before the alter and stood before Mary and the Child in his tunic, so thin that it was little better than a shift.

"Sweet Lady," said he, "to your protection I give myself. Scorn not the only thing I know, for with the help of God I will try to serve in the only way I can. How to chant or how to read to you I know not. All I can do is set before you my best tricks. I shall be like a bull calf that leaps and bounds before its mother. Whatever I am I shall be for you."

He began to turn somersaults, now high, now low, first forward, then backward.

Then he started to juggle his hoops and then his apples, and then his hoops and apples together, all the time balancing a stick on the tip of his nose. Then, as the chants of the monks rose louder from the church, he tumbled and leaped and turned gaily his somersaults and walked on his two hands, all the while juggling his rings and apples until he fell exhausted at the feet of the statue. Finally, with a humble heart, he raised his face.

"Sweet Lady," he said, "this I do for you and for your Son. I can do no more." Then he sighed, for he knew not how else to pray. "The others chant your praises in the church but I will return each day to this chapel to entertain you with my tricks."

Still looking at the image, he dressed himself and went his way.

In this manner many days passed. Barnaby went each day into the little chapel. Never was he too tired to do his best to entertain the Mother and Child.

Now, of course, the brothers knew that the boy went every day to the little chapel but no one knew, save God, what he did there. Nor did he wish that any of his goings and doings should be seen, for he believed, that were his secret once discovered he would be chased from the cloister and sent back again to the cold world.

The time came when Christmas was but two days away. On that very day one of the monks who had noticed Barnaby's absence from Mass decided to keep watch on him. So he watched and spied and followed until he saw the boy plying his trade in the little chapel.

"By my faith," whispered the monk to himself, "here is fine sport! Methinks that the sins of all the rest of us put together cannot equal this. While the others are at prayer and work, this tumbler dances proudly in the chapel. Thus he repays us. We chant for him and he tumbles for us! Would that the brothers could see him with their very own eyes, as I do this moment. Not a soul, methinks, could keep from laughing at the sight of this little fool killing himself with somersaults."

With these words he went at once to the Abbot and told him all from beginning to end. Thereupon the Abbot rose to his feet and said to the monk: "Now, I bid you hold your peace and do not tell this tale against your little brother. The next time he goes to the chapel we will go together. I would not have the boy blamed since he knows no better."

The next night, on Christmas Eve, the monks came to the little chapel with the beautiful gifts for the Christ Child and His Mother. Barnaby, with a sad heart, watched as each of the brothers laid his offering at the feet of the statue.

"Ah, sweet Lady," he sighed, "if only I could match the splendour of their gifts. Alas, I cannot."

When the service was over and the monks had returned to their cells, Barnaby crept back to the chapel, unnoticed by all save the spying monk and Abbot. These two went quietly and hid themselves hard by the alter in a nook where he could not see them. Barnaby bowed to the statue and laid aside his robe. The monk and the

Abbot saw his somersaults, his merry leaping and dancing, how he capered and juggled and walked on his two hands before the image until he was near fainting. This night, the birthday of the Christ Child, Barnaby worked harder and with greater skill than he had ever done before. When he had done, so weary was he, that he sank to the ground. There he lay all worn out.

Suddenly, while the Abbot and the prying monk looked, they saw descend from the statue's niche a Dame more glorious than any man had ever seen before, richly crowned and beautiful. Her garments were shining with gold and precious stones. Around her were the angles from heaven above. They drew close about the little boy. The Lady Mary took a white napkin and fanned her tumbler with it. Gently she fanned his neck and face and body and gave herself to the care of him. Then she returned to the niche above, but before she went she bent and kissed her little juggler.

Then was the spying monk filled with shame. His confusion made him glow like fire.

"Mercy, Sire. I have judged the boy wrongly. He is indeed a saint."

Barnaby heard not their whispers. Having finished his tricks, he dressed himself and joyfully went his way.

And so it came to pass that on the day after Christmas the Abbot sent for Barnaby, and the boy was greatly troubled.

"Alas, I am found out. Ah me, what shall I do? What shall I say? I do naught that is right. Woe is me. Surely they will bid me be gone."

He came before the Abbot with tears still wet on his cheeks and knelt upon the ground.

"Will you send me from your door, Sire? Tell me what you would have me do, and I shall do it."

Then replied the Abbot: "Answer me truly. Many weeks have you lived here. What service have you given and how have you earned your bread?"

"Sire," said the boy, "well knew I that I should be sent upon my way as soon as my doings were known. Now I will go. Miserable am I, and miserable shall I be, for I do naught to deserve my bread."

Then the Abbot raised him and kissed his two eyes.

"Little brother," said he, "hold now your peace, for I promise you that you shall stay here always. You and I

will be true friends. And now, dear brother, I command you to do this service — just as you did before — but openly and as well as you know how."

"Sire, is this truly so?"

"Yes," said the Abbot, "yes, truly."

So, very cheerfully and with still greater skill, did Barnaby continue to ply his craft for the Christ Child and His Mother. Cheerfully did he tumble and cheerfully did he serve.

Hazelnut Christmas cake

This is a quick and simple recipe, but with the rich ingredients it makes an effective alternative to the traditional Christmas Cake.

❖ 250 g (9 oz) ground hazelnuts
   200 g (7 oz) sugar
   2 teaspoons natural vanilla essence
   $^1/_2$ teaspoon almond essence
   250 g (9 oz) plain white flour
   4 level teaspoons baking powder
   1 cup of milk
   25 g (1 oz) plain chocolate (grated)
   icing sugar/ powdered sugar to decorate

Pre-heat oven at Gas Mark 4, (180°C, 350°F). Mix all the dry ingredients together. Add the vanilla and almond essence. Add the milk. The dough should fall off the spoon slowly. If it is stiff, add a little more milk.

Transfer the dough to a 20 cm cake tin lined with baking paper/oiled baking parchment.

Bake in the oven for 1 hour and 30 minutes. If the cake tin is larger the baking time should be reduced. Remove cake from oven and place on cooling rack. Sprinkle with grated chocolate while the cake is still warm.

Allow to cool for 15 minutes, then sprinkle with icing sugar and decorate with a sprig of holly.

We Wish You a Merry Christmas

Traditional

1,4 We wish you a Merry Christ - mas, We
2 Now bring us some fig - gy pud - ding, Now
3 We won't go un - til we get some, We

wish you a Mer-ry Christ-mas, We wish you a Mer-ry
bring us some fig-gy pud-ding, Now bring us some fig-gy
won't go un - til we get some, We won't go un - til we

Christ - mas And a Hap - py New Year!
pud - ding, And a cup of good cheer.
get some, So___ bring it all here.

1-3 Good tid-ings we bring To you and your kin. We

wish you a Mer-ry Christ-mas And a Hap-py New Year!

Christmas Time

It is a good idea to spread the excitement of Christmas over the twelve days, December 25 to January 5. It can be enough to have one present each on Christmas day and save the rest for Boxing Day, or even Epiphany. Again the children can be woken by a song on Christmas Morning. The Nativity set can be admired, and the final door of the calendar opened (if that has not already been done on Christmas Eve). The Advent wreath has now been put away.

Christmas is always the time to spend with relatives and friends, play games and enjoy the fresh air out of doors, but there is still plenty of time for crafts and baking.

German lebkuchen

❖ *2 eggs*
 180–200 g (7 oz) caster sugar
 1 teaspoon vanilla essence
 $^1/_2$ teaspoon ground cloves
 1 teaspoon ground Chinaman
 2 teaspoons rum
 2 teaspoons lemon juice
 lemon rind of half an unwaxed lemon
 $^1/_2$ teaspoon baking powder
 75 g (3 oz) mixed fruit peel
 125 g (4$^1/_2$ oz) ground almonds
 100 g (3$^1/_2$ oz) ground hazelnuts
 Rice-paper
 100 g (3$^1/_2$ oz) icing sugar/powdered sugar dissolved in lemon juice for topping.

Pre-heat oven at Gas Mark 4, (180°C, 350°F). Beat eggs and slowly add sugar until thick. Stir in the spices, vanilla essence, rum, lemon juice and lemon rind. Carefully add mixed fruit peel, ground almonds and baking powder, and finally the hazelnuts. Mixture should fall slowly off the spoon.

Lightly oil 2 baking trays and place rice-paper on top. Place small dollops of dough onto the rice paper.

Bake for 25–30 minutes. The outside should be turning golden, but the centre should still be fairly soft.

While the Lebkuchen are hot, brush them with the lemon icing to form a glaze.

Lemon hearts and cinnamon stars

These two traditional German Christmas cookies are best baked on the same day, as the one uses egg yokes and the other egg whites.

Lemon hearts

❖ *3 egg yokes*
 120 g (4 oz) sugar
 1 teaspoon natural vanilla essence
 2 teaspoons lemon juice
 lemon rind of half an unwaxed lemon
 $^1/_2$ teaspoon baking powder
 200–250 g (7–9 oz) ground almonds
 Icing sugar/powdered sugar and juice of half a lemon for glazing

Round for Four Voices

From Luther's hymn *Vom Himmel hoch*
Scots translation c. 1545

David Johnson

1. My soul and life stand up and see

2. Wha ly-is in ane crib of tree:

3. What babe is that, sae gude and fair?

4. It is Christ, God-dis son and heir.

Cinnamon stars

❖ *3 egg whites*
250 g (9 oz) icing sugar/powdered sugar
2 teaspoons natural vanilla essence
¹/₂ teaspoon almond essence
1 teaspoon ground cinnamon
275–325 g (10–11¹/₂ oz) ground hazelnuts

Pre-heat oven at Gas Mark 3, (165°C, 325°F). Beat egg whites until stiff. Slowly add the icing sugar, beating all the time. Remove 4 tablespoons and set aside. Add vanilla and almond essence, and the cinnamon. Stir in half the hazelnuts, and then gradually keep adding the remaining hazelnuts until the dough looses its stickiness, but remains soft and light.

Carefully roll the dough out ¹/₂ cm (¹/₄ in) thick, cut the stars out, and place them on a baking paper or oiled trays.

Using a brush or teaspoon coat each star with a little of the set aside icing mixture. Silver bobbles can also look festive and will stand up to heat.

Bake cookies for 15–20 minutes. The centre of the star should still be soft.

Pre-heat oven at Gas Mark 3, (165°C, 325°F). Beat egg yokes and sugar until thick and creamy. Add vanilla essence, lemon juice, lemon rind and baking powder. Stir in and almonds until dough is sticky and then knead the remainder, leaving enough ground almonds to roll out the dough, (icing sugar/powdered sugar can also be used for rolling out.)

The dough should be rolled out thin. Cut the hearts out and place them on a tray lined with baking paper or oiled grease-proof paper.

Bake in the oven for 10–15 minutes. If the cookies bake unevenly, the tray can be turned round in the oven after 5 minutes. Hearts should be whitish-golden when they are done.

Using a small bowl, add enough icing sugar to the lemon juice, so that it will be easy to brush on to the hearts when they come out of the oven. This should be done immediately to give an opaque glaze.

The Elves and the Shoemaker

From Grimms' fairy tales

A shoemaker, by no fault of his own, had become so poor
that at last he had nothing left but leather for one pair
of shoes. So in the evening, he cut out the shoes which
he wished to begin to make the next morning, and as he
had a good conscience, he lay down quietly in his bed,
commended himself to God, and fell asleep. In the
morning, after he had said his prayers, and was just
going to sit down to work, the two shoes stood quite finished on his table. He was astounded, and knew not

what to think. He took the shoes in his hands to observe
them closer, and they were so neatly made, with not one
bad stitch in them, that it was just as if they were in-
tended as a masterpiece. Before long, a buyer came in,
and as the shoes pleased him so well, he paid more for
them than was customary, and, with the money, the
shoemaker was able to purchase leather for two pairs of
shoes. He cut them out at night, and next morning was
about to set to work with fresh courage; but he had no
need to do so, for, when he got up, they were already
made, and buyers also were not wanting, who gave him
money enough to buy leather for four pairs of shoes.
Again the following morning he found the four pairs
made; and so it went on constantly, what he put out in
the evening was finished by the morning, so that he soon
had his honest independence again, and at last became a
wealthy man.

Now it befell that one evening not long before Christmas, when the man had been cutting out, he said to his
wife, before going to bed: "What think you if we were to
stay up tonight to see who it is that lends us this helping
hand?" The woman liked the idea, and lighted a candle,

and then they hid themselves in a corner of the room, behind some clothes which were hanging up there, and watched. When it was midnight, two pretty little naked men came, sat down by the shoemaker's table, took all the work which was put out before them and began to stitch, and sew, and hammer, so skilfully and so quickly with their little fingers that the shoemaker could not avert his eyes for astonishment. They did not stop until all was done, and stood finished on the table, and then they ran quickly away.

Next morning the woman said; "The little men have made us rich, and we really must show that we are grateful for it. They ran about so, and have nothing on, and must be cold. I'll tell you what I'll do: I will make them little shirts, coats, and vests, and trousers, and knit both of them a pair of stockings, and you make them two little pairs of shoes." The man said: "I shall be very glad to do it"; and one night, when everything was ready, they laid their presents all together on the table instead of the cut out work, and then concealed themselves to see how the little men would behave. At midnight they came bounding in, and wanted to get to work at once, but as they did not find any leather cut out, but only the pretty little articles of clothing, they were at first astonished, and then they showed intense delight. They dressed themselves with the greatest rapidity, put on the beautiful clothes, and sang:

"Now we are boys so fine to see,
Why should we longer cobblers be?"

Then they danced and skipped and leapt over chairs and benches. At last they danced out of doors. From that time forth they came no more, but as long as the shoemaker lived all went well with him, and all his efforts prospered.

Woollen angel

❖ *Teased sheep's wool, about 45 cm (18 in) in length*
Thin gold or silver thread

When working with teased sheep's wool do not cut it but pull it apart.

Separate off one third of the wool for the arms and wings of the angel.

1 Tie a knot in the middle of the thicker skein and pull it tight. This becomes the face.

2 Hold the skein vertically letting the wool above the knot fall down. Spread this wool round the head as hair and secure at the neck with a long gold thread.

3 Tie the ends of the gold thread together to make a loop for suspending the figure.

4 Lay the angel face down. Take the wool which you have just brought down for hair and divide it into three parts. Bring the middle part back up over the head, bring the other two parts to the sides - they will shortly become the wings.

5 For one of the arms separate off a bit of wool about 15 cm (6 in) long from the thin skein. Twist the wool firmly together in the middle, fold the skein double and tie up the hand with gold thread. Do not cut off the fluff forming the arms. Make the other arm in the same way.

6 With the angel still face downwards, place the arms under the neck and bring the tuft of wool which you laid over the head fall down over the arms. Turn the angel over, push the arms and wings well up, and tie up the body firmly under the arms with a length of gold thread. Allow the ends to hang down as tassels from the belt.

7 Fluff the wings and robe into shape by holding the wool firmly in one hand and teasing it out carefully with the other.

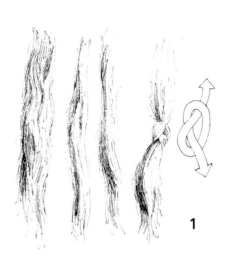

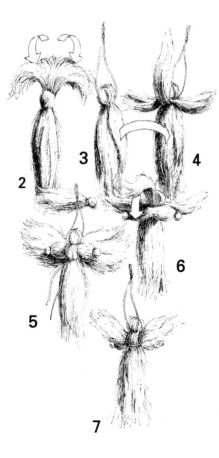

Window stars

Transparent stars are made by folding either square or rectangular pieces of transparent paper into a single star-point and then assembling these single star-points to make a star.

To make transparent stars use kite-paper or tissue-paper.

Kite-paper (transparency paper) is sufficiently transparent and is more robust than translucent tissue-paper, so it is more easily worked.

Tissue-paper is less colour-fast than kite-paper and since transparent stars are usually left to hang for a long time, tissue-paper stars can quickly lose their colour in sunlight.

The pattern in transparent stars emerges from the different layers of paper laid upon each other. In the more complicated star-points there can be up to eight layers of paper, so for complicated stars take pale colours otherwise the pattern will not be discernible.

Take great care that all the cut-out pieces are exactly the same size. It is also important to fold the sheets as exactly as possible because any divergence is magnified in the final result.

The crease must be really sharp.

When the same points have to be

Deck the Halls

Traditional, Wales

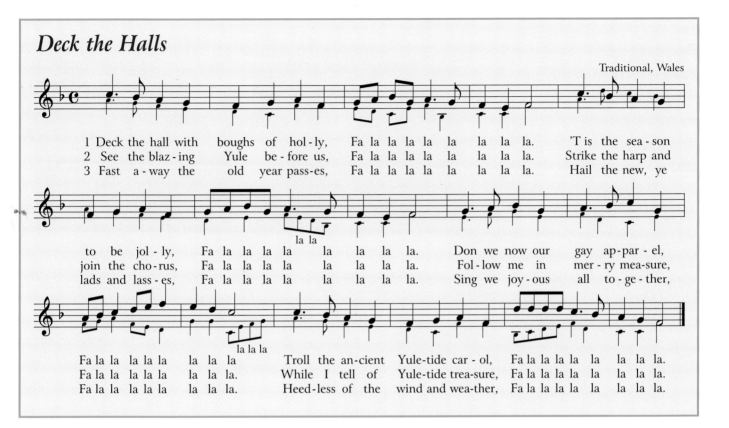

1 Deck the hall with   boughs of hol - ly,   Fa la la la la la   la la la.   'T is the sea - son
2 See the blaz - ing   Yule be - fore us,   Fa la la la la la   la la la.   Strike the harp and
3 Fast a - way the   old year pass - es,   Fa la la la la la   la la la.   Hail the new, ye

la la

to be jol - ly,   Fa la la la la   la la la la.   Don we now our   gay ap-par - el,
join the cho - rus,   Fa la la la la   la la la la.   Fol - low me in   mer - ry mea-sure,
lads and lass - es,   Fa la la la la   la la la la.   Sing we joy - ous   all to - ge - ther,

la la la

Fa la la la la la   la la la   Troll the an-cient   Yule-tide car - ol,   Fa la la la la la   la la la.
Fa la la la la la   la la la.   While I tell of   Yule-tide trea-sure,   Fa la la la la la   la la la.
Fa la la la la la   la la la.   Heed-less of the   wind and wea-ther,   Fa la la la la la   la la la.

Begin my Singers

Traditional

Be - gin, be - gin, my   sin - gers all, Let   voi - ces sound in   cho - rus.   In

har - mo - ny we   fill the_ hall, What   great - er pleas - ure   for_____ us.   We_

greet you well this_   Christ - mas time And   make this lit_ tle   can - on rhyme.

folded twice then do not make the first fold come exactly to the centre-line but allow a tiny space in between. Ensure that the sides come exactly together with the second fold.

Stick all the folded pieces together with a little transparent glue, adhesive or glue-stick. Non-transparent adhesive becomes visible immediately when the star is hung up.

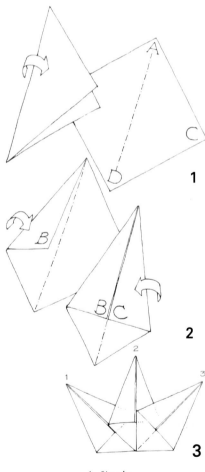

A Simple eight-pointed star

A. Simple eight-pointed star

❖ *8 squares 7.5 × 7.5 cm (3 × 3 in)*

1 Fold the sheets across the diagonal so that *B* and *C* meet. Unfold again.
2 Fold sides *AB* and *AC* inwards to lie along the diagonal. Stick them down with a spot of glue. Fold all the star-points in this way.
3 Stick the star carefully together, sticking the unfolded bottom *(D)* of the second star-point to diagonal of the first. Continue in this way until all the star-points have been stuck together.

B. Ten-pointed star

❖ *10 squares 7.5 × 7.5 cm (3 × 3 in)*

The previous eight-pointed star was simple to fold. A slight alteration in folding will change the motif of the star.

At the second stage make an extra fold opening the two flaps with the points *B* and *C* again and divide them into two, then fold them in again and stick them down.

Taking ten instead of eight folded points you can make the ten-pointed star. First make a five-pointed star. The overlap of each individual point is much less than half and in this way a pattern of rays appears in the middle.

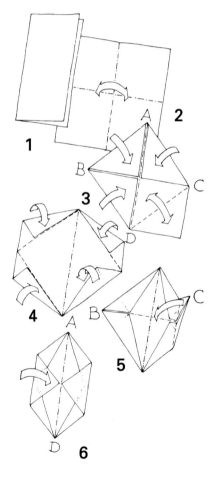

C Another eight-pointed star

Then add another five points exactly in between. In this way a splendid ten-pointed star will appear.

C. Another eight-pointed star

❖ *8 squares 10 × 10 cm (4 × 4 in)*

For this star rather larger pieces will be used because all the variations which follow have an extra fold.

1 First fold the pieces in two and then open them out again.
2 Turn the pieces round a quarter turn and fold them again across.
3 Fold the points of the square to the middle to make the square *ABCD*. Open the points out again.
4 Halve the triangles which have appeared and fold them again to the middle. This leaves a hollow diamond in the middle.
5 Then fold points *A* and *D* to the centre so that the lines *AB* and *BD* lie along the diagonal *BC*.

6 Stick the star-points together by sticking the second on to the diagonal of the first, and so on.

D. Simple eight-pointed star

❖ *8 rectangles 10 × 7.5 cm (4 × 3 in)*

With this star made of rectangles the long centre-line is the central fold.
1 Fold over the pieces lengthwise and open them up again.
2 Fold the four corners inwards to the centre-line to make a point at the top and bottom. Stick the corners down with a bit of glue.
3 Fold from the top point A the two sides again to the centre-line. This sharp point forms one of the points of the star, while the wider lower point comes into the centre of the star.
4 Stick the star together by sticking the second point on to the diagonal of the first, and so on (as for star A, p.84).

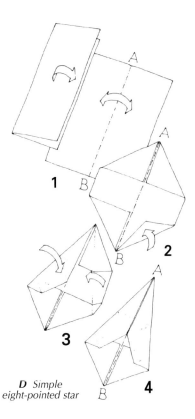

D Simple eight-pointed star

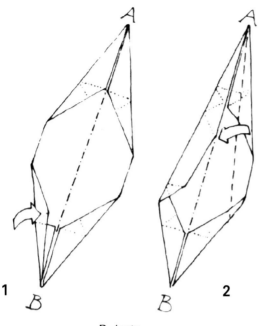

1   2

D *Acute
sixteen-pointed star*

E

E. Acute sixteen-pointed star

❖ *16 rectangles 15 × 4.5 cm (6 × 1³/₄ in)
(The diameter of star 30 cm, 12 in)*

In this star an extra fold is added and
so we take a larger size of paper.
1 Fold the star-points in the same way
as described for the previous star.
2 Now first fold the sides from the
bottom point to the centre-line.
3 Then fold the sides from the top
point to the centre-line.

Stick two points together as shown
in the figure for Star A (p.84 left,
No.3) and stick the third point between the first two. Stick the fourth
point on to the third, and the fifth
again between the third and the
fourth, and so on.

Because many layers of paper are
folded and stuck over each other it is
important to take a light-coloured
transparent paper.

Rose windows

❖ *White tissue paper
Coloured tissue paper
Non-drip adhesive (avoid liquid
    adhesive)
Pencil
Scissors (fine handwork scissors, or
    slightly curved nail-scissors)
Paper clips
Transparent contact paper*

Take a sheet of white tissue paper and
any other appropriate colours for the
chosen design.

Lay the sheets on top of each other
with the white sheet on top.

Hold them together with paper
clips.

Take a round bowl or tin, place it
ion the tissue papers and with a pencil
draw around the bowl.

Remove the bowl and cut out the
circles of tissue paper as accurately as

possible. If necessary it can be
trimmed later.

The white circle of tissue paper
serves as a foundation.

The remaining four circles must
each be folded as follows.
1 Fold in half
2 Fold in half again
3 Fold in half again, holding together
the edges which want to spring
apart.
4 Fold in half again (to a sixteenth
of the original size) but this time
fold half of the bundle upwards
and flip the other half downwards.

It is important to be very pre-
cise with these folds, with the
creases running to an exact point
and the sides pressed down flat, as
it affects the symmetry of the finished article.

From now on these folded pieces
will be called *wedges*.

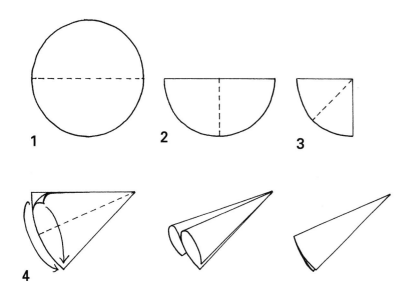

1 **2** **3** **4**

Do the same with the red wedge and then with the dark red one.

Trim the circle if necessary and then carefully place it onto the transparent contact paper. Cover the reverse side with contact paper as well.

Petal with hearts
This one is a little more complex, and needs precision to ensure the pattern lines up.

Lay the four wedges beside each other so that they make quarter of a circle with the lightest colour (first layer) on the left, then the second layer and the third; and finally the darkest on the right. Mark the seam allowance on this wedge.

Simple leaf
Mark the leaf-like curved line onto the wedges which you have in front of you. Cut along this line on each wedge.

Unfold the yellow wedge, smoothing out the creases as you unfold.

Now glue the yellow circle onto the white circle (only a small amount of glue is needed to hold the tissue paper in place).

Unfold the orange wedge and smooth it out. Make sure *all* the creases lie *exactly* on top of each other. It does not matter whether the crease is facing up or down (mountain or valley), but what is important is that the creases which belong to the pattern lie on top of each other. Once the second layer is correctly positioned it can be glued in place.

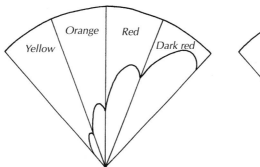

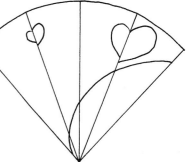

Star

With the next two examples, the pattern is cut out. This is done by cutting into the sides of the wedges, as in the patterns shown.

The star consists of only three colours (plus the white background).

Copy the pattern onto each wedge, then with a fine pair of scissors cut out the hatched part, taking care not to accidently cut through the arms.

Unfold the wedges fold by fold and smooth out, taking care with the delicate points.

First glue the lighter colour onto the white background. Lay the darker colour on top. Align and stick it at the edge.

Rosette

Rosettes are more intricate, but the results are stunning. The method is the same as for the Star.

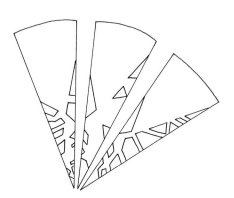

Good King Wenceslas

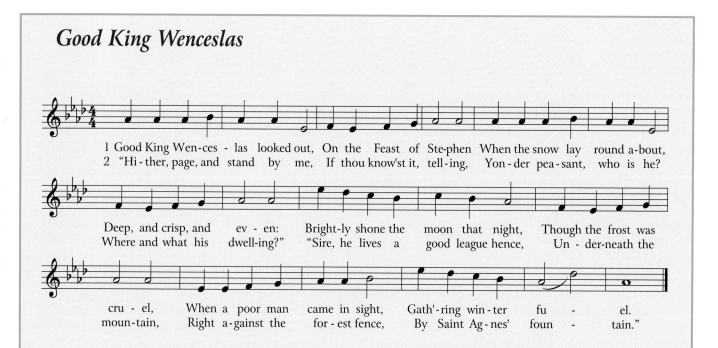

1 Good King Wen-ces - las looked out, On the Feast of Ste-phen When the snow lay round a-bout,
2 "Hi - ther, page, and stand by me, If thou know'st it, tell-ing, Yon - der pea-sant, who is he?

Deep, and crisp, and ev - en: Bright-ly shone the moon that night, Though the frost was
Where and what his dwell-ing?" "Sire, he lives a good league hence, Un - der-neath the

cru - el, When a poor man came in sight, Gath'-ring win - ter fu - el.
moun-tain, Right a-gainst the for - est fence, By Saint Ag - nes' foun - tain."

3. "Bring me flesh and bring me wine,
   Bring me pine logs hither;
   Thou and I will see him dine,
   When we bear them thither."
   Page and monarch forth they went,
   Forth they went together,
   Through the rude wind's wild lament
   And the bitter weather.

4. "Sire the night grows darker now,
   And the wind blows stronger,
   Fails my heart I know not how;
   I can go no longer,"
   "Mark my footsteps good my page;
   Tread thou in the boldly:
   Thou shalt find the winter's rage
   Freeze thy blood less coldly."

5. In his master's steps he trod,
   Where the snow lay dinted.
   Heat was in the very sod
   Which the saint had printed.
   Therefore, Christian men, be sure,
   Wealth or rank possessing,
   Ye who now will bless the poor,
   Shall yourselves find blessing.

89

New Year

It is not always possible for young children to stay up till the midnight hour, so for them, and all the family, a small celebration on the afternoon of New Year's Day can work very well.

The following is a suggestion.

Place a fairly large tub in the sitting room and organize the children to fill it with water. Make small boats out of hollow, split walnut shells. Fix a cake candle inside the bottom of each boat with melted wax. Ensure the boat floats well. Make one boat for each member participating — and a spare.

Write fortunes (one or two adult members should do this) on identical pieces of paper (a fortune for each participant — and a spare). Fold the paper into a strip. Bend the strips over the rim of the tub at regular intervals. When everyone has gathered round the tub, the youngest can take a boat, light their mast from a big candle by the tub and carefully place the boat in the middle of the water. The child can then choose a carol to be sung while the boat slowly makes its way to the edge of the tub. This usually happens by itself, but occasionally the water may

need agitating. The boat will come to rest at or near one of the papers.

The paper is then removed and the fortune read for that child. The process is then repeated for all the family, from youngest to oldest.

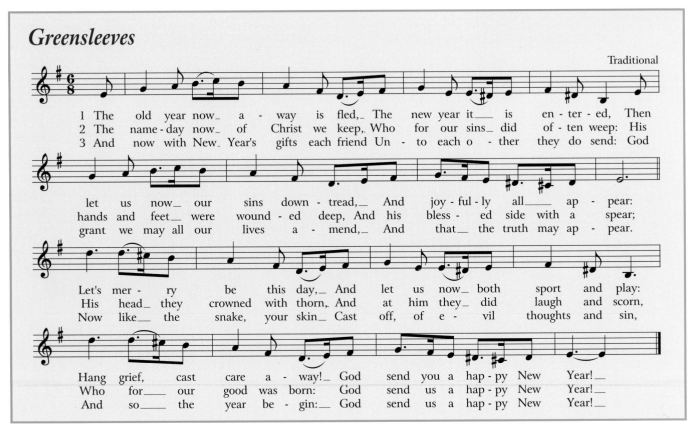

Greensleeves

Traditional

1 The old year now away is fled, The new year it is en-ter-ed, Then
2 The name-day now of Christ we keep, Who for our sins did of-ten weep: His
3 And now with New Year's gifts each friend Un-to each o-ther they do send: God

let us now our sins down-tread, And joy-ful-ly all ap-pear:
hands and feet were wound-ed deep, And his bless-ed side with a spear;
grant we may all our lives a-mend, And that the truth may ap-pear.

Let's mer-ry be this day, And let us now both sport and play:
His head they crowned with thorn, And at him they did laugh and scorn,
Now like the snake, your skin Cast off, of e-vil thoughts and sin,

Hang grief, cast care a-way! God send you a hap-py New Year!
Who for our good was born: God send us a hap-py New Year!
And so the year be-gin: God send us a hap-py New Year!

Wassailing Song

Traditional, Yorkshire

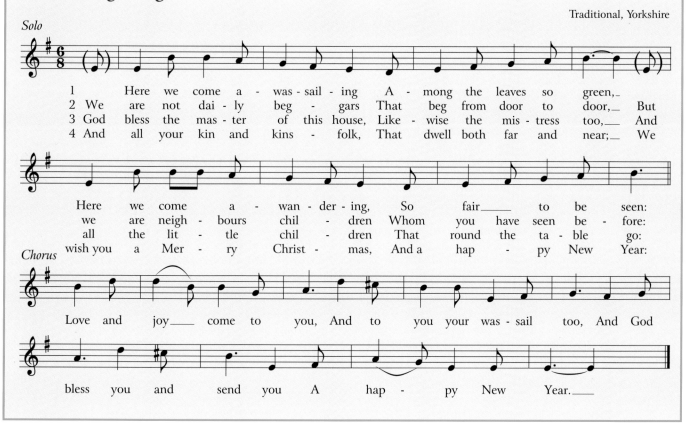

Solo

1 Here we come a - was-sail-ing A - mong the leaves so green,_
2 We are not dai - ly beg - gars That beg from door to door,_ But
3 God bless the mas-ter of this house, Like - wise the mis - tress too,_ And
4 And all your kin and kins - folk, That dwell both far and near;_ We

Here we come a - wan-der-ing, So fair___ to be seen:
we are neigh - bours chil - dren Whom you have seen be - fore:
all the lit - tle chil - dren That round the ta - ble go:
wish you a Mer - ry Christ - mas, And a hap - py New Year:

Chorus

Love and joy___ come to you, And to you your was - sail too, And God

bless you and send you A hap - py New Year.___

Mary Rocks the Baby

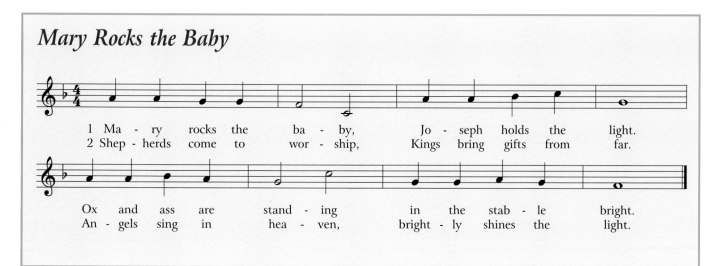

1 Ma - ry rocks the ba - by, Jo - seph holds the light.
2 Shep - herds come to wor - ship, Kings bring gifts from far.

Ox and ass are stand - ing in the stab - le bright.
An - gels sing in hea - ven, bright - ly shines the light.

The Stones of Plouvenic

In the village of Plouvenic there once lived a young stonecutter whose name was Bernet. He loved a beautiful girl called Madeleine, and wanted to marry her. But Bernet was very poor. Madeleine's father, a farmer, did not want a poor son-in-law, and he would not consent to the marriage. You shall hear how Bernet was able to marry Madeleine after all.

One Christmas Eve, while the farmer was feasting his men, there came a knock on the door, and outside in the cold wind stood an old vagabond who asked for shelter for the night. He looked a sly, artful old rogue, but because it was Christmas Eve, he was made welcome and given a place by the fire. After supper the farmer took him out to the stable and said that he might sleep there, on a pile of straw. In the stable were the ox who drew the farmer's plough and the donkey who carried to market whatever the farmer had to sell.

The vagabond was just falling asleep when midnight struck, and as everyone knows, at midnight on Christmas Eve all the beasts in a stable can speak to each other, in memory of that first Christmas in the stable at Bethlehem.

"How goes it with you, old friend?" the Ox asked the Donkey.

"Times are hard and I have been overworked," replied the Donkey.

"If only our master were richer," said the Ox, "he could buy more oxen and donkeys to lighten our load."

"If only he could find the treasure that lies under the Stones of Plouvenic!" brayed the Donkey.

"What treasure is that, my long-eared friend?"

"Why, you know those tall stones that stand in a circle on the hill beyond the village?"

"Yes, I know them. Each one is so big that it would take a team of oxen to drag it from its place."

"Well, under the stones there lies much gold. Once in every hundred years, on New Year's Eve at midnight, the stones leave their places and go down to drink at the river. They are gone for a few moments only; then they roll back to guard the gold again. A week from tonight they will leave their places to do this."

"If only our master knew that!"

"He would never return alive if he tried to get the treasure," said the Donkey. "The stones would come back and crush him before he had time to escape with it. He would be safe only if he could find a five-leafed clover, and carry that with him."

"Then all he need do is to find a five-leafed clover. Surely our master could do that if he looked hard enough."

"No, there is something else. Even if he escaped from the stones with the gold, it would crumble to dust at sunrise unless a human life were given in exchange for it."

The Ox sighed when he heard this. "Then there is no hope of our master or anyone else becoming rich that way. No one would give a human life in exchange for gold."

After this the animals fell silent. The vagabond lying in the straw, was very excited by what he had overheard. He thought how wonderful it would be just to see and touch the gold, even if it did turn to dust afterwards.

The next morning, he began to seek a five-leafed clover. There were only seven days before the stones would leave their places to drink at the river. He looked everywhere: in the fields, over the hill, in woods and hedgerows. And on the seventh day he found what he was looking for.

That evening, as the sun went down, he came to the hill where the tall stones of Plouvenic stood against the

gleamed in the moonlight. The two men ran forward and began to fill the sacks with the gold. A few moments went by, then tall shadows fell over the hilltop. The ground shook underfoot.

"The stones are returning!" Bernet cried in fear. "They will crush us!"

The vagabond laughed. "They will crush you, my friend, but not me."

As the stones rolled nearer, bearing swiftly down on him, the vagabond held up his five-leafed clover. At once the stones changed their direction and rolled towards Bernet. But what was this? Suddenly the largest stone of all, upon which Bernet had carved the holy cross, place itself before him as a shield. The other stones rolled back into their places. Bernet was saved.

Meanwhile, the vagabond had flung the sacks of gold over his shoulder and was staggering down the hill with them, chuckling to think how well his plan had worked. Then he heard a noise behind him. He looked round, terrified. The stone with the cross upon it was rolling after him! He held up his five-leafed clover, but its power was useless now. The stone rolled over him.

Bernet was left with all the gold for himself. He was now the richest man in Plouvenic. Madeleine's father gladly agreed that he should marry his daughter, and so the young stonecutter achieved his heart's wish, and he and Madeleine lived happily ever after.

sky. As he drew near the circle, he heard the sound of a chisel striking stone. Bernet, the young stonecutter, was there, carving a cross on the largest stone of all.

"What are you doing?" asked the vagabond.

Bernet smiled. "The times are hard, and no one has any work to give me. I am keeping my hand in by carving a cross upon this stone.

As he watched Bernet, a terrible idea entered the vagabond's head. Why should he not sacrifice Bernet to the stones, and so prevent the gold from turning to dust after he had taken it away? In a moment, the idea became a plan of action. The cunning vagabond told Bernet about the treasure. He told him that at midnight all the stones would go down to drink at the river, leaving the gold unguarded. But he did not tell him that they would be gone only for a few moments. Nor did he mention the five-leafed clover, or say that a human life must be given in exchange for the gold.

"I am old and feeble," said the vagabond. "You are young and strong. Help me to carry away the treasure in these sacks, and we will share it between us."

Bernet agreed to this plan very willingly. At last, he thought, he would be able to marry the beautiful Madeleine. Soon he would be a rich man!

Together Bernet and the vagabond waited on the hill. At midnight, the great stones began to rock and stir. Slowly at first, then gathering speed, they left their places and rolled down the hill to the river. And where the largest stone of all had stood, a great heap of gold

Caramel almonds

This very simple, quick recipe makes a tasty snack to enjoy on New Year's Eve.

❖ *100 g (4 oz) almonds*
100 g (4 oz) sugar
¹/₄ cup of water.

Prepare a tray lined with baking paper/baking parchment. Put all the ingredients into a milk pan and place the pan on a high heat. Bring the mixture to the boil, then stir constantly until the liquid has reduced. The sugar may crystallize, but keep stirring until the almonds are coated with a sticky, clear brown caramel — this will take 5 to 10 minutes.

Turn the contents out onto the tray and using two forks, separate the almonds as much as possible. This has to be done very quickly as the caramel soon hardens.

Once the almonds have cooled off, they can also be broken away from each other.

Nutty truffles

The quality of the truffle depends largely on the quality of the chocolate used.

❖ *100 g (4 oz) plain or milk chocolate*
40 g (1¹/₂ oz) butter
1 round tablespoon thick cream
1 teaspoon natural vanilla essence
6 round tablespoons ground almonds
2 round tablespoons icing sugar/powdered sugar
3 round tablespoons chopped/roasted hazelnuts
2 round tablespoons desiccated coconut/shredded coconut
desiccated coconut/shredded coconut for coating.

Gently melt the chocolate and butter in a double boiler. Remove from heat. Stir in the cream and vanilla essence. Mix in remaining ingredients and transfer to a lunch box.

Chill in the freezer for 1 hour (fridge for 8 hours) or until the mixture is firm enough to be rolled into balls.

Place the desiccated coconut/shredded coconut for coating on a plate and roll the balls in it.

Chill the truffles for a further 1 hour in the freezer (or 8 hours in the fridge) and then store in an airtight container in a cool place.

Makes about 30 truffles.

Peace and Goodwill

An eight-part round

Sing   peace   and   good   will,   sing   peace   and   good   will,   sing   peace,   sing peace.   Ring   out   through   the   air.   Now   shout   ev'-ry-where,   sing   peace,   sing   peace.

O'er the Hill and o'er the Vale

1 O'er the hill and o'er the vale,
Car - ing nought for snow and hail,
Come three Kings to - ge - ther.
Cold and wind and weath - er
Now on Per - sia's san - dy plains Now where Ti - gris swells with rains,
They their ca - mels te - ther: Now thro' Sy - rian lands they go, Now thro' Mo - ab faint and slow, Now o'er E - dom's heath - er.

Epiphany

Epiphany falls on January 6 and lasts until Candlemas on February 2. It is the festival of the kings.

The last day of Christmas is January 5, and yet the kings, too, belong to the time of Christmas. The two festivals can be joined in the mind of the child by introducing the kings a little earlier. They can start their journey after New Year and day by day work their way towards the nativity set. The shepherds have since returned to their fields. The kings can either arrive on the eve of Epiphany or Epiphany itself. The advantage with having a celebration on the eve is that the Christmas Tree can still be a part of it. The Bible reading from St Matthew (2:1–23) tells the story of the kings.

2. O'er the hill and o'er the vale
Each king bears a present
Wise men go a child to hail,
Monarchs seek a peasant:
And a star in front proceeds,
Over rocks and rivers leads,
Shines with beam incessant:
Therefore onward, onward still!
Ford and stream and climb the hill:
Love makes all things pleasant.

3. He is God we go to meet,
Therefore incense proffer:
He is King ye go to greet;
Gold is in your offer:
Also Man, he comes to share,
Ev'ry woe that man can bear -
Tempter, railer, scoffer:
Therefore now against the day,
In the grave when Him they lay,
Myrrh ye also offer.

Again, looking at relevant pictures will be helpful for the young child in following the language of the Bible.

It is especially meaningful if a representation of the gifts can be experienced by the children: a gold coin or ring to be looked at and felt; frankincense sprinkled on hot charcoal to be smelled, and myrrh (mixed with a little hot water) to be tasted (on the end of a finger, as it is very bitter). These gifts can then be placed at the nativity scene while the kings' carols are sung.

If the day of Epiphany is on a schoolday, the early morning can be made special by having a festive breakfast with coloured candles and the Epiphany loaf with its hidden treasure. The Christmas tree has been removed and the decorations put away for another year, although the kings, of course, remain.

There is a feeling of a new time in the year beginning.

Epiphany breakfast loaf with treasure

It is a tradition in many countries to celebrate Epiphany with a cake of some sort that has a hidden treasure within. The person who receives the treasure in their portion is allowed to be King/Queen for the day and choose a partner to rule with ...

This loaf is best for breakfast.

❖ *1¹/₂ teaspoons sugar*
280 ml (9 fl oz) mixed warm water and milk
3 teaspoons dried yeast
500 g (1 lb 2 oz) plain flour
1 teaspoon salt
75 g (3 oz) butter
75 g (3 oz) dried apricots (chopped)
75 g (3 oz) raisins
lemon rind of 1 lemon
2 small eggs lightly beaten.
110 g (4 oz) icing sugar/powdered sugar
lemon juice of half a lemon

50 g (2 oz) roasted, flaked almonds
silver and gold coated almonds
silver bobbles
treasure (such as a nut or a shiny penny wrapped in paper)

Dissolve the yeast and sugar in the warm milk and water and leave in a warm place for 10 minutes, or until frothy. Sieve the flour and salt into large mixing bowl. Rub in the butter. Mix in the apricots, raisins and lemon rind.

Form a well in the centre. Pour in the eggs and yeast liquid. Mix well and then knead on a floured surface until smooth and elastic. Cover with a cloth and leave for 5 minutes.

Divide the dough into two unequal parts. Take the larger part and divide it again into two.

Roll each half into a long sausage and then twist them together. On a lined or oiled baking tray form a circle with the twist.

Taking the smaller part, repeat the process and then place the smaller

twist carefully on top of the larger twist to form a round crown.

Leave in a warm place until the crown has risen to twice the size.

Pre-heat the oven at Gas Mark 7, (220°C, 425°F). Bake the loaf for 10 minutes at Gas Mark 7 and then reduce the heat to Gas Mark 5, (190°C, 375°F), and bake for a further 20–25 minutes.

Dissolve icing sugar/powdered sugar in lemon juice.

Remove the loaf from the oven, and place on a cooling rack.

While the loaf is still hot, make a small incision on the bottom and push the treasure inside. The hot dough will close round the treasure and hold it in place.

Then immediately glaze the top of the crown with the lemon icing, and sprinkle over with flaked almonds.

Use the lemon icing to stick the gold and silver decorations on.

Baboushka

All the villagers were out, bubbling with excitement.

"Did you see it again last night?"

"Of course we did."

"Much bigger."

"It was moving coming towards us. Tonight it will be high above us."

That night, excitement, like wind, scurried through the lanes and alleys.

"There's been a message."

"An army is on the way."

"Not an army — a procession."

"Horses and camels and treasures."

Now everyone was itching for news. No one could work. No one could stay indoors.

No one that is, but Baboushka. Baboushka had work to do — she always had. She swept, polished, scoured and shined. Her house was the best kept, best polished, best washed and painted. Her garden was beautiful, her cooking superb.

"All this fuss for a start!" she muttered. "I haven't time even to look. I'm so behind, I must work all night!"

So she missed the star at its most dazzling, high overhead. She missed the line of twinkling lights coming towards the village at dawn. She missed the sound of pipes and drums, the tinkling of bells getting louder. She missed the voices and whispers and then the sudden quiet of the villagers, and the footsteps coming up the path to her door. But the knocking! She couldn't miss that.

"Now what?" she demanded, opening the door.

Baboushka gaped in astonishment. There were three kings at her door! And a servant.

"My masters seek a place to rest," he said. "Yours is the best house in the village."

"You ... want to stay here?"

"It would only be till night falls and the star appears again."

Baboushka gulped. "Come in, then," she said.

How the king's eyes sparkled at the sight of the home-baked bread, the meat pies, the cakes, jams and pickles.

As she dashed about, serving them, Baboushka asked question after question.

"Have you come a long way?"

"Very far," said Caspar.

"And where are you going?"

"We're following the star," said Melchior.

"But where?"

They didn't know, they told her. But they believed that it would lead them, in the end, to a new-born king, a king such as the world had never seen before, a king of Earth and Heaven.

"Why don't you come with us?" said Balthasar. "Bring him a gift as we do. See I bring gold, and my colleagues bring frankincense and myrrh."

"Oh," said Baboushka. "I am not sure that he would welcome me. And as for a gift ..."

"This excellent black bread is fit for a king!" cried Balthasar.

Baboushka laughed. "Black bread? For a baby?"

Balthasar stopped her as she bustled once more to the kitchen.

"The new king could be your king, too. Come with us when the star appears tonight," he said.

"I'll ... I'll think about it," sighed Baboushka.

As the kings slept, Baboushka cleaned and tidied as quietly as she could. What a lot of extra work there was! And this new king. What a funny idea — to go off with the kings to find him. Yet, could she possibly do it? Leave home and go looking for him just like that?

Baboushka shook herself. No time for dreaming! All this washing-up, and putting away of dishes, and extra cooking. Anyway, how long would she be away? What would she wear? And what about gifts?

She sighed. "There is so much to do. The house will have to be cleaned when they've gone. I couldn't just leave it."

Suddenly it was night-time again. There was the star!

"Are you ready, Baboushka?"

"I'll ... I'll come tomorrow," Baboushka called. "I'll catch up. I must just tidy here, bake some more black bread, get ready ..."

The kings waved sadly. The star shone ahead. Baboushka ran back into the house, eager to get on with her work.

Sweeping, dusting, beating all the cushions and carpets, cleaning out the kitchen, cooking, baking — away went the night.

On and on she worked.

Baboushka looked through the window. It was dawn! Clear on the air came the sound of the farm cockerel. She looked up. The star had gone. The kings would have found somewhere else to rest by now. she would easily catch them up.

At the moment, though, she felt so tired. Surely she could rest now — just for an hour.

Suddenly, she was wide awake. It was dark. She had slept all day! She ran out into the street. No star. She rushed back into the house, pulled on her cloak, hurriedly packed her basket of black bread and stumbled down the path the kings had taken.

On she went, hurrying through village after village. Everywhere she asked after the kings.

"Oh yes," they told her, "we saw them. They went that way."

Days passed and Baboushka lost count. The villages grew bigger and became towns. But Baboushka never stopped, through night and day. Then she came to a city.

The palace! She thought. That's where the royal baby would be born.

"No royal baby here," said the palace guard

"Three kings? What about them?" asked Baboushka.

"Ah yes, they came. But they didn't stay long. They were soon on their journey."

"But where to?"

"Bethlehem, that was the place. I can't imagine why. It's a very poor place. But that's where they went."

She set off at once.

It was evening when Baboushka wearily arrived at Bethlehem. How many days had she been on the journey? She could not remember. And could this really

be the place for a royal baby? It didn't look like it. It was not much bigger than her own village. She went to the inn.

"Oh yes," said the landlord, "the kings were here, two days ago. There was great excitement. But they didn't even stay the night."

"And the baby?" Baboushka cried. "Was there a baby?"

"Yes," said the landlord, "there was. Those kings asked to see the baby, too."

When he saw the disappointment in Baboushka's eyes, he stopped.

"If you'd like to see where the baby was," he said quickly, "it was across the yard there. I couldn't offer the poor couple anything better at the time. My inn was packed full. They had to go in the stable."

Baboushka followed him across the yard.

"Here's the stable," he said. Then he left her.

"Baboushka?"

Someone was standing in the half-light of the doorway. He looked kindly at her. Perhaps he knew where the family had gone? She knew now that the baby king was the most important thing in the world to her.

"They have gone to Egypt, and safety," he told Baboushka. "And the kings have returned to their kingdoms another way. But one of them told me about you. I am sorry but, as you see, you are too late. The kings came as soon as they saw the star. It was Jesus the Christ Child they found, the world's Saviour."

"Ah me," sighed Baboushka, "I am too late, but I shall lay my black bread in the manger, then the Christ Child will know I came. I shall sleep here for the night and start home in the morning. Come, ox and ass, we shall sleep side by side tonight, for it is cold outside."

Soon Baboushka fell into a deep sleep only to be awakened by a beautiful golden light, which came form the far corner of the stable.

"Baboushka, Baboushka, I am here. Come rise and greet me," said a child's voice.

"Who are you?" cried Baboushka in fright.

"Do you not know, have you not been looking for me? I am the one they call the Christ Child."

"Oh Child, I have waited so long to see you."

"Then walk into my light, Baboushka, and let us hold hands," said the voice softly.

And Baboushka did so.

The next day they found old Baboushka dead, curled up on the straw, with only the ox and ass to watch over her.

But that is not quite the end of my story. For every Christmas Eve children all over Russia hang up their stockings in the hope that they will be full in the morning. And so they are, with toys and games, and right at the bottom in coloured paper is a piece of black bread. The old ones who know, nod their heads and say Mother Christmas has been there. "See, Baboushka has left some black bread. Just as she did for the Christ Child all those years ago."

We Three Kings

1 We three kings of O-ri-ent are: Bear-ing gifts we tra-verse a-far
5 Glo-rious now, be-hold him a-rise, King, and God, and sac-ri-fice!

Field and foun-tain, moor and moun-tain, Fol-low-ing yon-der star:
Heav'n sings al-le-lu-ya, Al-le-lu-ya the earth re-plies:

Refrain after each verse

O___ star of won-der, star of night, Star with roy-al beau-ty

bright, West-ward lead-ing, still pro-ceed-ing, Guide us to thy per-fect light.

2 Born a king on Beth-le-hem plain, Gold I bring, to crown him a-gain.
3 Frank-in-cense to of-fer have I; In-cense owns a de-i-ty nigh:
4 Myrrh is mine; its bit-ter per-fume Breathes a life of gath-er-ing gloom;

King for e-ver, ceas-ing nev-er, O-ver us all to reign:
Prayer and prais-ing, all men rais-ing, Wor-ship him, God most high:
Sorrow-ing, sigh-ing, bleed-ing, dy-ing, Sealed in the stone-cold tomb:

Cookie cutter candles

❖ wax
   wax crayon stubs of different colours
   candle wick (if old candle ends are used,
      extra wick will not be necessary)
   small cookie cutters
   jam jar
   small pan
   tray lined with aluminium foil

Place the wax in the glass jar (if old candle ends are being used, remove the black tip of the wick beforehand).

Colour the wax by adding a crayon stub of choice. Fill the pan half full with water and place the glass jar in the middle. Heat the pan until the water is nearly boiling, then reduce the heat to maintain a constant temperature.

While the wax is melting, ensure the tray is level, and the cutters have no holes or gaps in them. If they do, block the spaces with Blutack from the outside, then place the cutters on the foil.

When the wax has melted, remove the old wicks, straighten them out, and allow them to cool on the foil. If new wick is being used, cut it to the appropriate size and dip it in the melted wax to harden it.

Lift the glass jar out of the pan, drying the bottom with a towel to avoid water drips, and pour the wax into the cutters, filling them half full. Two people will be needed for this: one to hold the cutter down firmly onto the surface to stop the wax leaking out, and the other to pour the wax, taking care not to burn the helper's fingers.

Continue to hold the cutter down for a further 20 seconds and then fill the cutter full. Allow the wax to set for about half a minute and then push the wick into the centre. If the wick falls over, allow the wax to set longer.

Leave the candles for about an hour and then gently ease them from their moulds.

If this cannot be done, place the candles in the freezer for 15 minutes and try again. The candles should come out easily from the cutters.

Candle dipping

Hand-dipping candles is a very simple and satisfying craft for children. Beeswax candles are particularly lovely to burn at the children's bed-time throughout Epiphany.

❖ small saucepan
   tin or glass jar
   wax
   wick

Fill the saucepan half full with water. Fill the tin/jar with wax and place it in the centre of the saucepan. Heat the saucepan until the water is about to boil and then reduce the heat.

As the wax starts to melt, the tin/jar may need to be topped up with more wax. The dipped candle will be just as long as the depth of melted wax.

When the wax has completely melted, cut an appropriate length of wick and dip it into the wax. Using finger and thumb to straighten the wick.

Allow the wax to cool before dipping again (about 15 seconds). Dipping should be done quickly, so the wax building up on the candle does not have time to remelt.

Wax drops will build up at the base

Oaken Leaves

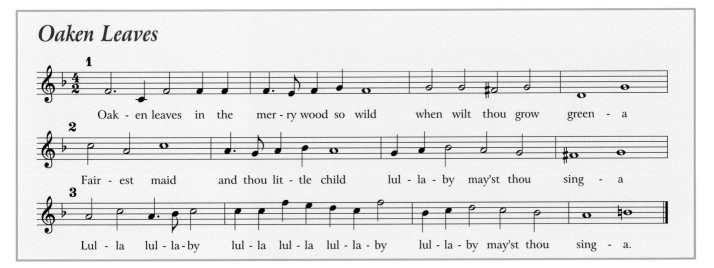

1 Oak - en leaves in the mer - ry wood so wild when wilt thou grow green - a

2 Fair - est maid and thou lit - tle child lul - la - by may'st thou sing - a

3 Lul - la lul - la - by lul - la lul - la lul - la - by lul - la - by may'st thou sing - a.

Three Kings in Great Glory

Allegro *Soprano solo* *Chorus* *Solo*

p

1 Three kings in great glo - ry of hor - ses and men, Of hor - ses and men, In____
2 Come mon - archs, and en - ter, your Mon - arch is here, Your Mon - arch is here, Doff__
3 Then sim - ple and gen - tle, and fool - ish and wise, And fool - ish and wise, Come a -

Chorus *Solo*

p

haste come a - rid - ing o'er moun - tain and fen, O'er moun - tain and fen; For their
crowns, on the bare sod fall down and re - vere, Fall down and re - vere; For the
dore the great Lord of the earth and the skies, The earth and the skies, Who__

Chorus *Solo*

p

King is a - wait - ing, and lo they would bring, And lo they would bring, The__
best you can of - fer is lit - tle, I trow, Is lit - tle, I trow, To the
deigns for us all on this night to be born, This night to be born, This__

Chorus

p

best of their trea - sure to give to their King, To give to their King.
Lord God of heav'n you're a - kneel - ing to now, A - kneel - ing to now.
night that is fair - er than mid - sum - mer morn, Than mid - sum - mer morn.

of the candle and should be cut off with a knife from time to time. The wax can then be put back in to the tin to melt again.

When the candle is as fat as desired, hang it up to cool and harden for at least an hour. The candle can also be laid on foil to harden.

Daz candle holders

❖ *Daz — or similar modelling clay*
  straight drinking glass or small
    rolling pin
  knife
  paint
  varnish
  glue (PVA adhesive is particularly suit-
    able because it acts as a varnish as
    well as a glue. It is also non-toxic and
    washes off clothes etc, even when dry.)

Daz clay does not require any kneading before use. Basic candle holders can be made either from a ball, or from rolling the daz out flat and cutting a shape out.

A long snake can also be made and wound round to an appropriate shape.

Children enjoy making all sorts of accessories to stick on at a later stage: plaits, balls and shapes of all kinds. The Daz will slowly dry out while being handled, so it is best to complete the design within an hour.

Place the holders on a plate and leave them in a warm, dry place. They make take several days to dry out completely.

When dry the holders can be painted with simple water colours.

After the glue/varnish has been applied the accessories can be stuck on.

Kings from Far Away

1 Kings from far a - way lands we are. Cas - par Mel - chi - or Bal - tha - zar
2 We have tra - vell'd through ma - ny lands Val - leys, moun - tain - tops, des - ert sands.

Star of Beth - le - hem light of Beth - le - hem guide our wan - der - ings gold - en star.
Pre - cious of - fer - ings King - ly of - fer - ings Ho - ly of - fer - ings in our hands.

Acknowledgments

The author and publisher would like to thank the following:
— Christofoor Publishers for instructions and pictures from *The Christmas Craft Book* by Thomas Berger: Straw stars (p. 25), Straw ball (p. 26), Gold-foil angel (p. 65), Woollen angel (p.82)
— Thomas Berger for the window stars (pp. 82-97) from his booklet, *Window Stars*
— David Johnson for his round "My Soul and Life" (p.79).
— Tom Rosenberg for the sstory of St Nicholas (p.20)

Every effort has been made to identify the authors of all the stories, songs and carols, but this has not always been possible. Apologies to anyone whose name has been omitted, we will be happy to amend these in any future edition.

Index